GHOST HUNTING

HOW TO INVESTIGATE
THE PARANORMAL

BY LOYD AUERBACH

PROFESSOR PARANORMAL

RONIN PUBLISHING

BERKELEY, CALIFORNIA

Ghost Hunting

Copyright 20044by Loyd Auerbach

ISBN: 1-57951-067-1

Published by

Ronin Publishing, Inc.

PO Box 3436

Oakland,CA 94609

www.roninpub.com

Production:

Editor:	Beverly Potter	docpotter.com
Cover Design:	Brian Groppe	
Cover Photos:	Jonathan Postal	
Book Design:	Beverly Potter	

Fonts:

Brutality, Jakob Fischer/PizzaDude, pizzadude.cjb.net

Gouty Old Style, URW Software

Nightmare, Astigmatic One Eye Foundy, astigmatic.com

Palatino, Apple Computer

Tussle, 2001 Iconian Fonts, iconian.com

Library of Congress Card Number: 2003098086

Distributed to the book trade by **Publishers Group West**

Printed in the United States by **Avarto Services, div Bertelsmann**

ACKNOWLEDGMENTS

I'S BEEN A NUMBER OF YEARS since I wrote my first book, ESP, Hauntings, and Poltergeist. Since then, a few people wo were influential in my life have died, and hopefully gone on to another existence. It's important for me to acknowledge them, not just for their contributions to my parapsychological career, but also for their extensive contributions to the field of parapsychology: Dr. Karlis Osis, Alex Tanous, D. Scott Rogo, Marcello Truzzi, and Martin Caidin. I wish there was more room to say something about each one.

Since publication of *ESP, Hauntings, and Poltergeists*, there have been so many additional people who have made an impact on me, my perspectives on the paranormal, and on this book's future. Many have been named in the acknowledgments of my other books. Listing them here would take many pages. I want to apologize for not doing so.

There are a few people I will acknowledge here and now: Pamela Heath, Annette Martin, David Richardson, Beverly Potter, Phyllis Galde, Jill and Travis Mahoney-Banks, Shawn Hendricks, Laura Green, Dave Manganelli, John Riggs, Mark Garetz, Neva Turnock, and everyone who's ever worked on my investigations with me...and those who are part of the new Paranormal Research Organization.

And most of all, my wife, Julie Levin, who has believed in me and supported me in this and so many other projects.

There are many, many others...thank you all for everything.

DEDICATION

THIS BOOK IS DEDICATED...

To the memory and spirit of Marcello Truzzi. I always appreciated his wit and wisdom, but I didn't really grasp the impact he had on my life and my career until after he was gone.

To the paranormal investigators out there who are looking for the how and why, trying to fit the answers to the right questions.

To Julie ,most of all, who keeps me happy and tolerates my books and stuff. I love you.

BOOKS BY LOYD AUERBACH

ESP, Hauntings and Poltergeists:
A Parapsychologist's Handbook

Reincarnation, Channeling and Possession:
A Parapsychologist's Handbook

Psychic Dreaming:
A Parapsychologist's Handbook

Mind Over Matter:
A Comprehensive Guide to Discovering
Your Psychic Powers

TABLE OF CONTENTS

INTRODUCTION

A N INTENSIVE FORMAL EDUCATION is not necessary to become a well-rounded, knowledgeable, and ethical paranormal investigator or field researcher. What is necessary is an understanding of what the field of parapsychology tells us about investigative techniques that work, what the phenomena are, and how to help people deal with them. A solid knowledge base is necessary for any real investigation, and even more necessary if your interest lies in helping people resolve these cases.

In *Ghost Hunting* you'll find clear techniques for investigating different types of phenomena, as well as discussion of the technology that has and hasn't been useful. You'll find out why most professional investigators place more stock in the human experience than in any technology.

Ghost Hunting is not about running around with cameras, meters, and audio recorders looking for orbs, vortices, magnetic fields, and spirit voices. It's about understanding what's going on in the individual cases and in general. It's about the *ghost story*—the experience and what it means. And mostly it's about helping people through their experiences.

Ghost Hunting will start you off on the path towards becoming a knowledgeable, ethical, and reliable field investigator and researcher. It will give you a broad picture of the thought processes a paranormal investigator goes through, so that you, too, can start conducting investigations.

Ghost Hunting is for those well into the paranormal and provides techniques to approach a situation so as to best understand what is and isn't happening, what is and isn't paranormal, and how to take the next step to "remove" the phenomena, if that's what is called for.

Ghost Hunting will help cut through misconceptions about investigating reports of ghosts and poltergeists, from the "evil spirit" myths to the "spirit orbs" concept. Many books purport to tell you how to conduct investigations. Only a couple provide a solid basis in what parapsychologists have learned over the last 100-plus years. You will discover that there are many explanations for the orbs, voices, and energy fields detected and recorded. You will learn that there's much more to these cases, much more that's interesting and even exciting, than what one might capture on film or tape or digital media. *Ghost Hunting* will educate and motivate the legions of new ghost-hunters out there to rethink what you're doing and guide you in becoming real investigators, looking for what's *really* happening.

Whether you are a believer, nonbeliever, or somewhere in between, *Ghost Hunting* is meant to enlighten you as to what people do experience and what paranormal investigators are really up to. It's meant to impress upon you the importance of keeping an open mind while at the same time questioning reports of psychic happenings, looking for the separation of the normal from the paranormal. It's meant to entertain you. It will guide you to become a paranormal investigator and field researcher who knows what you're doing!

PROFESSOR PARANORMAL

1

PARAPSYCHOLOGY

HE WORD GHOST MEANS MANY THINGS to many people in different cultures and religions. For the most part, the word has come to mean something—or someone existing without a body, yet can be perceived by us living folks. For the most part, the word is associated with living people and animals who die—sometimes called spirits—and survive the death of the body. However, *ghost* has also been applied to disembodied beings who were never alive, such as demons and angels from some religions and mythologies.

APPARITIONS

I LIMIT THE USE OF THE TERM GHOSTS to the more common application of spirits of the dead, or as they have been called in parapsychology and psychical research before it, *apparitions*, which are quite different from *hauntings* or *poltergeists*.

Understanding the concepts surrounding psychic experience and abilities is important, since they are essential parts of our modern models of ghostly happenings. Telepathy and psychokinetic abilities enable one to "see" or communicate with ghosts and for ghosts or poltergeists to be able to move objects. Let me lay some track for your journey to becoming a knowledgeable paranormal investigator.

A DEFINITION

PARAPSYCHOLOGY IS THE STUDY of psychic or *psi* phenomena, pronounced "sigh." It studies exchanges of information between living things, mainly people, or between living things and the environment, as well as influences of living things on the environment, which occur without the use of what we call the "normal" senses, and do not seem to be explicable by the currently accepted physical laws of nature. I use the term *psi* interchangeably with *psychic*.

Parapsychology as a science has to do with connections and consciousness—or mind. Not merely content with mainstream concepts of how the mind works in general, parapsychologists want to know if consciousness has other channels of information flow than the normal senses, whether it can connect with the minds of others, if it can reach out and affect the world directly, and if it can survive the death of the body. It's all about consciousness, but in terms of connection, interconnectedness, and existence aside from the body.

NOT PARANORMAL

THE EXISTENCE OF A MIND-SEPARATE-FROM-BODY may not be necessary for most psychic experience, but it sure is for ghosts. For such experiences to happen *in the way they are reported*—rather than the way they are defined—there is not a necessity for the outside existence of consciousness. Even for apparition cases, there are alternative psychic explanations that don't rely on after-death survival, as you'll see.

Author investigating the psychic abilities of the aborigine in the outback of Australia with psychic Suzane Myles.

Parapsychologists give more credibility to mind/consciousness than many in other sciences do. The experiences we study are grouped into three main categories.

Paranormal psychology, if it were to exist as a recognized subfield of psychology, would involve looking at the psychology of paranormal experiences and belief systems. While there are some psychologists who do this, too many of them look at psi experiences and beliefs as "abnormal" and perhaps even indicative of mental aberration. In fact, simply having a psychic experience often points to a diagnosis of some kind of psychosis.

SIDEREAL TIME

OVER THE YEARS, PARAPSYCHOLOGISTS AND OTHERS doing lab research in this field have found ways the environment allows us all to be more or less psychic, seemingly enhancing our abilities. This may be a key factor in how we experience apparitions, hauntings, and poltergeists.

When it comes to having a psychic experience, whether seeing a ghost or having a premonition, it's been clear that a lack of other things going on can be key. We tend to notice things when the locale is quiet, with little activity or noise to distract us. That's why people may have more ghost sightings at night.

Some studies have suggested that there's a particular window in Local Sidereal Time, or LST, that allows people to be more psychically receptive. Sidereal Time is measured not by the rotation of the Earth around its axis or the position of the sun in the sky, but by looking at particular stars and constellations are overhead. The sidereal day is a few minutes shorter than our 24-hour solar day, so this window of about an hour around 13:30 LST shifts from day to day. In psi experiments people scored much higher during this window on tasks than at other times of day or night. There hasn't been a real attempt to correlate LST to hauntings as yet, but that's coming. As a point of interest, sidereal clock programs for your computer can be found in many places on the world wide web.

Author in the Outback.

2

ESP AND PK

HE FIRST GROUP OF PARANORMAL PHENOMENA has been called "receptive psi" or "informational psi." It is probably more familiar as ESP, or *Extra Sensory Perception*. Psychologist and psi researcher Keith Harary suggested a more descriptive phrase: *Extended* Sensory Perception. Researchers also use the phrase—*Anomalous Cognition*—or unexplained knowing. These experiences involve the transfer of information. There are several concepts relating to this form of psi.

TELEPATHY

TELEPATHY IS AN AWARENESS of information or emotions that exist in the mind of another. A simpler way of saying this is "mind-to-mind communication." Telepathy is not really reading someone's mind. The transfer of information often occurs spontaneously, or when you least expect it. Studies have indicated that it's fairly simple to block others from receiving information from your mind, and to block from your mind receiving thoughts of others.

CLAIRVOYANCE

CLAIRVOYANCE IS A FRENCH TERM meaning "clear seeing," and refers to the receiving of information from objects or events at the present time without the use of the normal senses or without piecing together things from clues you might have. Literally the term refers to visual information, but parapsychologists might include under this heading information that comes in as sound, physical sensation or smells.

REMOTE VIEWING

REMOTE VIEWING IS A PROCESS IN WHICH ONE PERSON is able to view what another person in a different location is looking at. It has also been called *remote perception* since psychically, one might receive information in the form of sounds, feelings, sensations, smells, or tastes. Today, most researchers use either remote viewing (RV) or anomalous cognition (AC).

PSYCHOMETRY

Psychometry can be listed under clairvoyance. It is the ability to read the history of an object or location, or gain information about the people associated with it. Some psychics say they receive information through the vibrations or energy an object or location gives off. One possibility is that all material objects actually can somehow record information, whether in the electromagnetic field that surrounds matter or through some other means, and that some people are able to decode that information.

In most respects, this is the main explanation for a *haunting*, where an apparition is seen or heard or felt to perform the same acts over and over, like a replay of past events. You may enter a so-called haunted house, pick up on the history of the location, and have your mind provide a replay of some of the events that happened there in the past.

When employing a psychometry-type model we can speculate that there is a real physical explanation for this form of ESP, one that may not need much reconciliation with our current models of physics and biology.

Another explanation for psychometry is that the object acts as a focus for the psi abilities of the person doing the reading, enabling the psychic to clairvoyantly locate appropriate information. This is why some psychics may request an item owned by a missing person before trying to locate that person. Tarot cards, crystal balls, and other occult items often serve as a focal point for a psychic to tune into something clairvoyantly.

PRECOGNITION

WHILE CLAIRVOYANCE DEALS WITH EVENTS OR OBJECTS in the present, the third skill, *precognition*, is the ability to receive information about objects or events that exist in some future time. Of all the psi abilities that parapsychologists study, precognition has always held the most fascination for humanity.

We're constantly hearing or reading about some psychic making a new prediction. One wonders why they aren't doing things like making money at the racetrack. Of all the psi abilities, precognition has the most uncertainty associated with it, since we really don't know whether information can cross Time, or if the Future is set enough to actually read what will happen.

Along with the ability to gain information through Time from the Future, is an ability called *retrocognition*, or awareness of objects and events that existed in the Past. The Past, unlike the Future, has already happened, so many people find this ability somewhat easier to understand. In fact, this proposed psi talent has been suggested as an alternative explanation for psychometry—and hauntings—in the sense that instead of reading the history of an object or location from some energy field, the person receiving the information is simply using that object or location as a focal point to look into the Past.

PSYCHOKINESIS

THE SECOND GROUP OF INTERACTIONS has been collectively referred to as expressive psi, or "mind over matter." Parapsychologists have applied the term *psychokinesis*, or PK to a wide range of effects and abilities. This is true mind over matter, the ability of the mind to influence material objects or processes without the use of known physical processes.

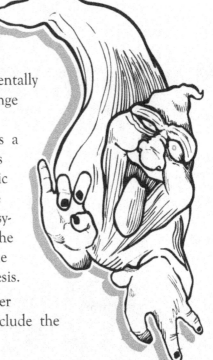

Psychokinesis covers a wide range of effects, although the one you're probably most familiar with is *telekinesis*, the ability to mentally move objects. This can range from simple up-and-down levitation to floating across a room or even flying across the sky. Since psychokinetic effects include much more than just levitation, parapsychologists have given up the older term *telekinesis* for the broader one of psychokinesis.

Besides telekinesis, other reported big PK effects include the materialization or dematerialization of objects, even apparent teleportation. There are reports of mental impressions having been put onto film or videotape, of film being fogged mentally, and of video tape erased with a mere thought. Such things have been investigated in the laboratory to some degree of success. Sounds have apparently been produced on audiotape as well.

POLTERGEIST

THE PK PHENOMENON AT ISSUE throughout this book is the *poltergeist* experience. In German the word literally means "noisy ghost." In poltergeist cases, objects are reported to move about under their own power, things break by themselves, sounds are heard, and perhaps some vague forms may even be seen lurking about. Parapsychologists link the experience to a living person or persons, and to stress-related situations. Because all events surround a central person called an *agent*. Most of the events follow a pattern, although the timing of the happenings is generally spontaneous. Because the events tend to recur, parapsychologist William G. Roll coined the phrase *Recurrent Spontaneous Psycho-Kinesis*, or RSPK, to cover this modern model of the poltergeist.

OTHER PK EFFECTS

PARAPSYCHOLOGISTS GROUP OTHER PHYSICAL EFFECTS under the PK label. *Psychic healing*—unusual healing of self or others that is mind-directed—is being studied by both parapsychologists and researchers in other fields.

Much research has been conducted in the area of human-machine interactions, looking at how the mind can affect computers and other electronics directly.

3

SURVIVAL

ENTRAL TO MANY BELIEF SYSTEMS about paranormal events is the concept of life after death or the "survival of bodily death," as parapsychologists like to put it—or simply *survival* This was the major area of investigation for the early psychical researchers.

APPARITIONS

APPARITIONS ARE A CENTRAL FOCUS in understanding the concept of "survival." An apparition is what is seen, heard, felt, or smelled representing that part of the human personality that can somehow exist in our physical universe after the death of a person's body. An apparition is a person's personality—the spirit, soul, consciousness, mind, or whatever you want to call it—that survives the death of the body. It is capable of *interaction* with the living and presumably other apparitions. If the "presence" has true personality or intelligence behind it, we consider it a true apparition, but if it doesn't display self-awareness and interactivity, it may simply be a haunting, which is an environmental recording.

A metaphor for this is a situation in which you enter a room with a video monitor. You see a friend on the monitor, and he begins talking to you. Now, this friend might be on a video conference system live, so the two of you can interact. But you could be viewing a videotaped message from that friend. A videotape is a representation of the friend, whereas a live connection indicates intelligence and interactivity.

CONSCIOUSNESS

IN LOOKING FOR EVIDENCE OF SURVIVAL, whatever consciousness is, it is different and separable from the brain and therefore the body. Some modern philosophers, physicists, parapsychologists, and psychics have postulated that consciousness is a result of some process of the brain which generates a field of energetic interactions, a field that may in fact be able to continue on after the death of that brain. More materialistic scientists and nonscientists believe that what we call our mind may be advanced "programming," or specialized subroutines programmed into the gray matter of our brain.

Can anyone *prove* that we humans have a mind, or a consciousness, at all—especially one different from animals or even "thinking" machines like computers? Not at this point. Is there a device we can point at or hook up to a person that would indicate or detect a mind? Brain scan devices, which only detect indications of activity in the brain, do not indicate that the mind is something separate from the physical brain.

We can't currently prove the existence of a mind *in* a body, where we assume there is a mind. We can't prove the existence of ghosts without first proving the existence of consciousness. Parapsychologists are caught in a kind of catch-22 because we can't expect to detect consciousness outside the body—where we are not sure it is—when we can't even detect the mind inside the brain where we assume it is.

Out of the Body

Psychic Annette Martin seeks spirit contact in Alcatraz, the now-closed prison.

While apparitions are a major indicator of consciousness surviving death, they are not an easy class of phenomena to study. Parapsychologists look at *out-of-the-body experience*—affectionately called an OBE. This is the sensation or experience many people have of actually leaving their body for a time. According to many psychics, it's not actually the soul or spirit that leaves the body, but just a part of the mind or consciousness that can split off and travel.

The indication that consciousness has some kind of separate ability to exist outside the body is key to the concept of survival. A number of OBEs have been connected to apparitional sightings, which, in this context, are *apparitions of the living*. Cases of apparitions of the living are fairly common, and an investigator must be aware that an OBE may be at the root of an apparitional sighting.

OBEs are a component of a classic *near-death experience*, or NDE, which is yet another experience of the living that implies survival of consciousness. An NDE occurs when a person is clinically dead for a brief time, then resuscitated. The person typically recalls having had various experiences while "dead," including seeing a tunnel with a light at the end of it.

MEDIUMSHIP

MEDIUMSHIP IS A KEY ELEMENT of the history of parapsychology, and can be important to the paranormal investigator. A medium is a person who serves as an intermediary between the physical world and that so-called plane of existence where the spirits of the dead reside. The medium is generally either at the center of the communications, or is the actual channel through which contact is made.

Until the late 20th Century, mediums were stereotyped as going into trance and getting in touch with their particular *control entity* who acts like an otherworldly telephone operator, to contact the lost loved one. Information from the departed person may come through in a variety of ways, from being poured directly through the mouth of the medium, being related to the medium by the originating spirit with the medium repeating the words to the living, or perhaps with the message told to the control, who relays it to the medium who then relays it to the living. Today, we'd call such folks *trance* mediums.

In the early 21ˢᵗ Century, several mediums have risen to popularity with their books and media appearances. However, these folks refer to themselves as *psychic* mediums, meaning they see, hear, or sense the spirits and their messages psychically, while still very conscious.

This label "medium" covers any psychics parapsychologists might work with who claim to be able to communicate with an apparition. Researchers into mediumship are looking at the connection to apparitional sightings.

REINCARNATION

PARAPSYCHOLOGISTS INCLUDE EVIDENCE for *reincarnation* in their research. The ancient idea of the spirit or soul reborn in another body is accepted in some form or another by a number of the world's many religions. Though reincarnation research findings certainly support the idea that consciousness survives death, it has little to do with cases of apparitions, hauntings, and poltergeists.

4

POLTERGEISTS

PHYSICAL EFFECTS ARE THE CENTRAL THEME in poltergeist cases. Noises such as rapping sounds or footsteps in the walls, floors, ceilings, or furniture are heard. Smaller objects slide across tables and shelves, or even launch themselves across the room, occasionally flying from one room to another, and often striking walls at the end of their flights. Pictures and other wall hangings may rotate, become dislodged, or take flight themselves. Heavier items, such as furniture, may begin to topple over or simply rearrange. Objects may disappear completely, or reappear in unusual places. Electrical items like lights and appliances may turn themselves on and off. The phone may work by itself. Computers may misbehave in ways that even software engineers or hardware specialists can't explain.

On rare occasions, small fires may break out, though not to any extent portrayed in film and television. Although rare, there may be visual apparitions, unusual sounds or perhaps voices, or strange smells without an apparent source, yet perceived by all present at the location.

Not all of these things happen in a typical poltergeist case, and most often the results of a poltergeist "attack" are more like kids running amok than the frightening images seen in horror movies.

TYPICAL CASE

THE TYPICAL POLTERGEIST (RSPK) CASE is one of limited duration, from a couple of weeks to perhaps as long as a year and a half. This contrasts with apparition cases, which vary greatly in duration, and with hauntings, which are related to the actual location and may last for many years, even centuries. There have been longer-term poltergeist cases lasting for several years, but they are rare.

TEMPER TANTRUM

PARAPSYCHOLOGISTS VIEW A POLTERGEIST as a situation caused by the subconscious mind of a *living agent*, generally someone in the household undergoing emotional and/or psychological stress. Typically agents are people who have no method of dealing with the stress in a normal manner, so the subconscious takes advantage of the psychokinetic ability we all have to blow off steam. You can think of the poltergeist scenario as a telekinetic temper tantrum.

The physical things affected can often be used as clues to determine what's bothering the poltergeist agent. The agent is identified by looking at who is around during the events. The objects affected may belong to a particular individual in the household, or be representative of a role of one of the family. For example, suppose a husband doesn't want his wife to work, asking her to stay home and effectively "in the kitchen." Kitchen appliances may act strangely when the subject of the wife working is brought up in discussion. Water bursts may be representative of pent-up guilt or grief.

On rare occasion, poltergeist cases have provided visual apparitions, though these are generally distorted, archetypal, or even monstrous. In other words, you don't get a basic human ghost, but a projection of stress, guilt, anger, fear, or frustration from the subconscious, which is telepathically sent out to others in the household.

EPILEPSY

SIGNS OF EPILEPSY OR EPILEPTIC-LIKE ACTIVITY were found in the brains of a significant percentage of a group of poltergeist agents given neurological examinations. One study yielded 33 percent with epilepsy-like activity. A hypothesis put forward is that for *some* people the RSPK may simply be another form of epileptic seizure. In some cases where such activity was found in the brain, agents felt "better" or "relieved" after an RSPK attack, or the RSPK occurred at times in which there were no seizures.

Regardless of how it manifests, people can be counseled or treated, and a poltergeist "busted" without occult mumbo-jumbo or even nuclear-powered particle accelerators.

ATTACKS

IN SOME RARE CASES, there is physical damage to an individual's body, such as scratches and bruises appearing with no apparent cause. Such incidents inevitably turn out to be caused by one of two things, and both are essentially the same. The first possibility is the fear reaction is so great that people harm themselves panic and become careless and clumsy. A second possibility is that the people being injured are the RSPK agents, whose subconscious minds direct the energy at their own bodies for some psychological reason, as in a psychosomatic illness. Of course, deception is also possible.

In one of my cases, a woman was unconsciously punishing herself because of some deep-seated psychological issues of which she was unaware. Her unconscious desire to bring them to the surface caused her to "see" a shadowy figure that would reach out and choke her. Bruises spontaneously appeared on her throat, sometimes in front of witnesses. I witnessed this myself.

Incidents where someone got hurt in a poltergeist case, bring up this bit of advice—Never ever duck *into* the path of a flying object! That's right, injuries in poltergeist cases are often caused by getting into the path of the objects, or more frequently losing balance because of surprise and/or fear.

When injuries or attacks are reported, one must be careful not to jump to any conclusions that the harm is caused by the poltergeist or by an outside entity. But how do we know it's not a ghost doing it?

AGENTS

THERE SIMPLY HASN'T BEEN A GOOD INDICA-TION of an outside agency causing the incidents in most cases, especially when they revolve around the presence of a living person in the situation. Even in cases where apparitions are seen, or sounds or voices with intelligence are heard, or unusual smells are perceived, the events generally point to a living person as the

agent, who is telepathically projecting or suggesting the appearance of the other perception-related incidents—the sounds, smells and so forth.

There are situations where the physical activity may be related to an actual apparition. Two California apparitional cases I've spent much time on over the years revolve around apparitions who have *learned* to move things. Both apparitions have been in their locations for decades, with the only discernible agents of the PK being the apparitions themselves.

ADOLESCENT • GENT

MOST CASES INVOLVE FAMILIES, although there have been workplace poltergeist cases. The causal stress may be related to family, school, or workplace interactions. Looking over a number of cases, we find that the agent is frequently an adolescent, though the sex of the agent may not matter. The agent-as-adolescent fits the stress paradigm, since the physical and emotional changes going on in the body of an adolescent are themselves sources of tension, frustration, and stress. Add in stress-causing interactions within the home or educational situation, and the stress builds up. The result may be a poltergeist, a case of RSPK.

Adolescence can continue into one's 20s. The adolescence connection is not always there, however. Some of us have had poltergeist agents as old as in their 60s and 70s, though almost never younger than 11.

MULTIPLE AGENTS

THE RSPK MODEL USUALLY POINTS TO A SINGLE AGENT, but it can include the interpersonal relationships that are going on, for example. The person pegged as the agent may be around without anything happening when the people or circumstances causing the tension, frustrations, and stresses are not also present. In fact, the very presence of an outsider, such as a parapsychological investigator, may upset the family dynamics enough to cause the phenomena to stop.

In most cases, the poltergeist agents are unaware of causing the incidents. For most of us, having PK means taking more personal responsibility for our thoughts and the actions that come from them. Most people have an issue with personal responsibility, so the phenomena generally stops once the person realizes the connection and accepts that responsibility.

One of the most interesting developments in viewing the poltergeist agent as the cause of the RSPK is the way in which some agents turn a negative experience into a positive one. Some agents who have taken the responsibility for the RSPK, owning up to the fact that the phenomena are caused by their own minds, have been led to turn the experience around by taking control of those abilities, if only for a short amount of time.

One interesting issue is that the phenomena *itself* can be an intense stress-point that helps escalate the RSPK. In other words, a little PK causes the people involved, especially the agent, to stress further, resulting in more unconscious PK.

GHOSTS AND PK

APPARITIONS DON'T HAVE PHYSICAL BODIES, yet by definition they are still capable of interacting with the physical world. No body means no hands or means of physically interacting in the way we living folks do. Thus interactions with the living must be through the apparition's mind affecting physical objects and processes, which is the definition of psychokinesis.

Therefore, if an apparition is indeed capable of such an interaction, some poltergeist cases could conceivably be caused by an invisible entity. However, there are usually no other indicators of an intelligent, interactive apparition in poltergeist cases. Also very telling is the fact that apparitional PK cases are never as physically active or chaotic or destructive as poltergeist cases.

There's one more difference between poltergeist and other cases. The phenomena may continue over many years or even decades associated with the presence of an apparition, even though the living people in the location have completely changed over time. Poltergeist cases tend to be short lived, almost always less than two years, often less than two months.

In apparition cases, the PK may not even begin for months or years after the ghost is seen, and may continue for as long as he or she is around. Many jump to the conclusion that an apparition is the cause in poltergeist cases. Put that consideration at the bottom of your list.

HAUNTINGS AND PK

HAUNTINGS MIGHT INCLUDE SPONTANEOUS PSYCHOKINETIC activity without any evidence of a ghost. Such cases may be mistaken for poltergeists. As a haunting is picked up by the minds of visitors to the location, it may be that the recording can set off the visitor's PK, thereby causing the occurrences to repeat with different visitors or apparent agents who are sensitive to it. The perception of the haunting may be the stress point that sets off a poltergeist agent.

Hauntings are often long term, going on for years, decades or even centuries. PK activity is rare in such cases. When it does occur, it's not connected to a single agent or family.

FRAUD

Magician Gerry Griffin uses trickery to make a pen appear to levitate.

WE MUST ALWAYS LOOK for motives and methods of fraudulently creating a poltergeist situation. In the typical poltergeist case, most families don't know how to pin down what's going on. So an unseen— and generally "evil"—unknown entity or ghost is blamed for the happenings. A psychologically or emotionally disturbed person in that situation may actually have created the poltergeist on their own, purposely moving of objects through purely physical means in order to act out the stresses and lash out at the family.

We have situations in which the conscious mind has begun imitating the unconscious PK. If the subconscious mind does these things to let off steam without drawing blame—"the ghost did it!"—the conscious mind could certainly recognize such possibilities. We ghost hunters have to watch out for both real and pseudo-poltergeist activity.

5

HAUNTINGS

NLIKE POLTERGEISTS, **where the phe-nomena is caused by the agent, a haunting is received by the witness. Hauntings** actually show that we are all psychic receivers to some degree. We've all had the experience of walk-ing into a house and getting a feel for its "vibes." While the feeling could be a result of normal perceptions, such as pleasing décor, you may be psychically perceiving emotions and events embedded in the environment.

In haunting cases, people report seeing, hearing, feeling, or even smelling one or more presences, which are typically engaged in some sort of activity. It could be a figure walking up and down the hallway, footsteps heard from the attic, a man and woman physically fighting until one is dead, or even the sounds of two people making love coming from an adjoining room as occurred in one of my more memorable cases.

The events and figures witnessed in hauntings tend to be repetitive both in what's experienced and the timing of the occurence. Speaking with the ghosts tends to do no good, because they just con-tinue to go about their business, as though you're not even there.

Some claim this is because the ghosts are "stuck" in some sort of cursed time loop. Hauntings have occurred on many occasions where the entities are representative of *living people*, in which there's no dead person to be stuck.

A RECORDING

WHAT DOES APPEAR TO BE STUCK is some kind of environmental recording of events and people. Like the small object that a medium may hold and read in psychometry, the house, building, or land somehow records its history, with more emotion-laden events and experiences coming through louder and stronger. That people mostly report negative events and emotions, such as those accompanying suicide, murder and other violent crimes, or emotional fights, is likely due to a reporting artifact rather than any unbalanced ratio of negative to positive events. If you experienced a haunting in which generally good feelings are picked up in the house, would you report it? Unlikely.

An imprint of a big 1940's party continues to replay at the Brookdale Lodge in Northern California.

The Brook Room at the Brookdale Lodge boasts a haunting with music and reverly.

Think of a haunting as a loop of video tape playing itself over and over for you to watch. Trying to interact with it would be akin to trying to interact with a show playing on your VCR. You can turn it off or change the tape to another movie; the actors wouldn't suddenly stop and converse with you.

Researchers have found that people oblivious to the haunting phenomena when they first enter the haunted site are likely to pick up something in the same spots in the house as the those primary witnesses who reported the haunting. This indicates that *something* actually exists in the environment at those spots on some level, physical or psychic.

An important consideration is whether the content of the replay is related to what's gone on in the house or on the land under it before the current building. Often it is possible to track the story back to events in the current or past inhabitants' lives.

HARMLESS

A HAUNTING IS A RECORDING, a memory of the place itself, and not something that has the capacity to harm anyone. People can screen out such things from their perceptions, ignoring them as they would road noise heard from within their houses. On the other hand, a repetition of a recorded bit of nastiness, such as a murder or suicide, can be more than just annoying and hard to screen out. It can be stressful and cause one to want to move out of the house.

PLACE CENTERED

HAUNTINGS ARE GENERALLY CENTERED IN ONE PLACE, rather than connected with any one person as with poltergeists, and have no expiration date. The events of a haunting seem independent of the people in the location, and rarely include the movement or influence of physical objects. Any psychokinesis in a haunting situation may be the result of the information received by the people from the haunted location or object setting off a burst of subconscious PK.

OBJECT CENTERED

As HOUSES ARE BIG OBJECTS, it's possible that small objects, such as furniture, toys, and jewelry can be haunted as well. In a number of cases, it has turned out that an antique in the home was the source of the recording that created the haunting.

PAST EVENTS

IT'S INTERESTING TO THINK OF HAUNTINGS as recordings
of past events. Patterns may be observed as to when
and under what conditions the events are seen, but
an investigator cannot really re-create those conditions. Conditions can be related to weather, times of
day, and perhaps even the tidal influences and
phases of the moon.

Not everyone who enters a haunted house or
other location experiences the events. It may be that
certain people have more sensitivity to the recordings,
so the phenomena may not be observed every time
the physical conditions are met. Throw in the possible influences of mood and belief of the observers,
and the perceptions can be affected even more.

Not everyone experiences the haunting the same
way, with the same perceptions. Some people may
have a visual experience, while for others the experience may be auditory. Some may smell or sense
something or even experience the proverbial cold
chill. Any combination of the above is possible.

Another explanation relates to the nature of Time
itself. It may be that what one sees when looking at
the image in a haunted location is the actual event
happening in its own time, as somehow witnesses
actually look back into the Past. Whether this is
because of some fluke in the setup of Space-Time
itself or whether it's due to retrocognitive ability is
unknown. Since not all people in the location experience the haunting, the Time problem is unlikely.
The haunting is most likely some process bringing in
recorded information from the location, or
retrocognition.

SLICE OF HISTORY

KEEP IN MIND that one is experiencing a piece of history, from years ago to the very recent. Think of it—you're experiencing something from the past! Imagine the possibilities. If we could control the playback ability, whether this is in the environment or in ourselves, or a combination of the two, imagine the possibilities. We could potentially observe historical events provided we were in the right location. Think of what this could add to our knowledge of history, or the ability of police to determine who committed a crime. Think of the entertainment value.

MAGNETIC FORCES

IN THE 1980s, Dr. Michael Persinger of Laurentian University in Canada began looking at how the magnetic field generated by the Earth might impact human beings and their behavior, specifically looking at connections between psychic experiences and changes in the local geomagnetic fields. Several correlations were found, indicating that as the Earth's magnetic field goes up and down, both globally and in a given area, people report varying types of psychic experiences.

Persinger delved further, looking at what parts of the brain might be affected. He found the greatest impact on the temporal lobes, which regulate some of our behaviors and emotional states. He created a helmet that can pulse magnetic fields of appropriate frequency and field strength in varying patterns into the brain. This causes the subject to have a variety of experiences, from those similar to near-death experiences or other mystical experiences, to hallucinations of alien abduction or apparitions.

Persinger's work suggests that the Earth's magnetic field or other natural EM fields may cause us to have hallucinatory experiences attributed to apparitions and hauntings. It is possible that the increasing magnetic energy in the environment is responsible for many such experiences.

MAGNETIC FIELDS

MANY PARAPSYCHOLOGICAL RESEARCHERS BEGAN MEASURING local magnetic fields in the late 1980s, when magnetic field detectors, or magnetometers, were becoming smaller and affordable. The devices measure magnetic fields given off by a variety of sources, including technology. They are useful in looking for correlations between where people experience hauntings and unusual magnetic field readings.

What's so interesting in haunting cases is that the spots where people experience the phenomena tend to have higher magnetic readings than the background, even with all household power turned off. Magnetometers measuring fields of a more natural frequency have also shown such correlations, even though there is no discernable cause for the fields.

Is the magnetic field indicative of the recording itself? We're not sure yet, since the use of magnetometers in haunting cases is still fairly new. Is the magnetic field an indication of something that *causes* an individual to be more psychic, and so pick up the recording? Again, we're not sure, but research by Persinger and others looking at the connections between the Earth's magnetic field and psi abilities, as well as the use of such fields to cause people to have hallucinations, is particularly promising.

NOT UNDERSTOOD

THERE'S A MAJOR PROBLEM with making such fields and mere hallucinations the explanatory cause of all of the experiences. Hauntings may indeed be hallucinations caused by magnetic fields. But the problem is that the theory is still incomplete if this is so. In hauntings, you can have verifiable hallucinations, dealing with the history of the object or location. These experiences take place over many years, with many witnesses unfamiliar with the history of the location or the haunting. Reports of extensive hauntings go back centuries, well before our modern technology began putting out ever more magnetic pollution.

Apparition cases also may provide verifiable information. This is not the case when using Persinger's magnetic helmet. While magnetic fields are definitely measured in our cases, and while they may be part of *why* the people have experiences of apparitions and hauntings, they cannot be pointed to as the actual cause of all the experiences, especially the more interactive, apparitional ones.

Magnetic fields in hauntings may be related to whatever in the environment holds the information or may make the witnesses more sensitive to the information. In any event, research shows there is a clear connection between magnetic fields, the brain, and our perceptions. Ghost hunters must consider such fields in all cases of apparitions and hauntings.

6

APPARITIONS

OLLS AND SURVEYS INDICATE that millions of people have had an apparitional encounter of some kind. The long-term apparition—one that sticks around for a while—is fairly rare, however.

Apparitions generally behave like normal, living, human beings. They appear with intelligence and intent, which differentiates them from hauntings, which are characterized by images of the past. Apparitions seem to be goal-oriented, with the goals—including communication and interaction—generally being those personal to the apparition.

LIKE A HOLOGRAM

GHOSTS DO NOT LOOK LIKE WHITE-SHEETED, cloudy figures, or green, hot-dog-gobbling figures or balls of light. In fact, the way an apparition appears is often more startling than what we heard in old ghost stories. Ghosts look like people, like you and me. They may be a bit fuzzy around the edges, out-of-focus, or a bit see-through. Generally, however, witnesses report that apparitions look quite solid and three-dimensional, much like a hologram. The figures of apparitions may run from the tops of the heads to just below the knees—feet are sometimes missing.

The apparitional form is generally the same form the person had in life. They react to people and surroundings in the same way a living person would. Their size and stature appear within normal bounds. They never seem to shrink or grow, although the age and physical appearance may reflect another period of that person's life, and may even change from time to time. In one case I worked on, the apparition was seen as a little girl, a teenager, and as the old woman she was at the time of her death.

SELF IMAGE

IN SOME ENCOUNTERS, you may not even realize you're looking at an apparition, unless the figure suddenly vanishes before your eyes, or you notice the feet missing. Besides appearing and disappearing mysteriously, these figures may exhibit other unusual behavior. They can apparently walk or transport themselves

*The Moss Beach Distillery in Northern California
is home to the ghostly Blue Lady*

through solid objects like walls and doors, or appear in midair as if levitating. How apparitions presents themselves seems to have to do with the apparitions' self-image.

Apparitions appear to have no particular form other than a projection of how they see themselves. In other words, how the rest of us see ghosts depends what they visualize for themselves.

Try this: Close your eyes and picture yourself in your mind's eye. That self-image probably how the living would see you if you wereis a ghost. Did you visualize yourself with clothing? Of course! Which is why ghosts very rarely appear nude: their self-images include clothing.

WHAT HAPPENS

MOST APPARITIONS ARE SEEN BY A RELATIVE, friend, or loved one—generally only once—within 48 hours of death, as if the person is saying good-bye. Apparitions may tie themselves to one location. In some cases the apparition followed the witnesses from place to place, probably because of a personal, emotional attachment to the witness.

Ghosts hang around where there are people: in homes, offices, and restaurants and bars. Reports of ghosts in cemeteries are extremely rare.

Most apparitions don't stick around as ghosts for more than a day or two. Longer-term apparitions tend to have a psychological need or strong desire to stay here, such as a denial of death, fear of "what's next," a strong desire to stay with loved ones, or even anger at a life cut short. Not everyone with strong desires or needs sticks around as an apparition, however.

The beach below the Moss Beach Distillery where a woman was murdered and later became the restaurant's ghost.

Certain environmental factors may allow people with strong desires or needs to stick around. I suspect these factors include both geomagnetic conditions and an unidentified factor in the physical environment.

RARELY THREATENING

FOLKLORE ABOUT GHOSTS CAN CAUSE PEOPLE'S FEARS to stop them from attempting to communication with the apparition. In many cultures and religions around the world, ghosts are thought to harbor ill will towards the living. This is unfortunate, since the evidence from thousands of cases of near-death experiences suggests that people don't change their personalities or motivation after death. They don't receive spiritual answers that make them smarter or wiser—nor do they turn evil.

Most human beings are basically decent, or at least neutral in life—and in death. Even in ghost cases where people report being injured, injuries are inevitably a result of fear of the ghost, which causes clumsiness or impairs decision-making. Researchers looking at evidence for survival and paranormal investigators have found little evidence that murderers or evil people hang around as ghosts.

There have been cases—including a few I've investigated—where the ghost was bitter or lonely or obnoxious or simply someone with poor self-esteem. Such apparitions can be verbally abusive or even downright insulting, and they can certainly play on the fears of the living.

INTERACTIVE

INTERACTION WITH AN APPARITION IS TWO-WAY. Consider how the apparition perceives your behavior towards it. You may become frightened and your reaction may frighten the apparition or hurt its feelings.

Should you encounter an apparition, don't be frightened, instead try to communicate with him. You have much more to fear from living intruders who may carry guns and knives than ghostly ones. Furthermore, you may have your own built-in psychic defense mechanisms. People are not seriously hurt in any of these cases, and there is rarely any harm done to an observer at all, unless the harm is caused by poor judgment resulting from panic.

EXPLANATIONS

THERE ARE FEW GOOD PHOTOS OF GHOSTS, and most are suspected of being produced though unintentional error—or fraud. When apparitions appear before two or more people, *not everyone sees them.* This suggests that no physical materialization is being seen. Nothing to reflect light means there is nothing to photograph. The conclusion—apparitions are telepathic projections into a witness' perception.

The prevailing hypothesis is that apparitions telepathically communicate and our mental processes pick up this self-image and add it to the information received by our normal senses. Some of us process telepathic input on a visual basis, others are auditory or sense through feeling or smell. Many experience a ghost on more than one perceptual level, such as both seeing and hearing the apparition. The perceptions of a ghost that we receive as witnesses are projected by the mind of the apparition—a telepathic message. So as observers we sees only what the apparition wants us to see.

ESP

ACCEPTING THE IDEA THAT A MIND, SOUL, OR SPIRIT is capable of existing separately from the body is necessary to consider the possibility of survival of bodily death.

Extrasensory perception may explain how a mind without a body can interact with living people or other disembodied minds. A ghost doesn't have a physical mouth or voice, so the only way it can convey a message is through telepathy. The message is transmitted from the mind of the ghost to the mind of the living person witnessing it.

PSYCHOKINESIS

Psychokinesis offers an explanation of how a disembodied entity can physically interact with a living person. If a mind can affect objects or events and if the mind can exist without the body, then we can envision that disembodied entity interacting physically through psychokinesis.

If something appears in a photo when a ghost is sensed or perceived, one explanation is that the apparition *intended* something to appear and used PK to affect the medium that recorded the image—the film or digital media. Another possibility is that the expectations of the photographer were responsible for the PK-created effect on the photo.

This underscores that an investigator *must* have an understanding of psychic functioning, scientific research methodology and findings in order to explain what might be going on.

Apparitions of the Living

NOT ALL GHOSTS REPRESENT DEAD FOLKS. There are thousands of cases in which apparitions seen at one location represent a living person *somewhere else*. Most cases are spontaneous and unintended by the person appearing as an apparition, such as in the midst of a dream, during an out-of-body experience (OBE), or when in physical danger. Some, however, are deliberate intentions to be seen, usually when in danger or gravely ill as a call for help, or during an OBE.

Investigating Sightings

GHOST CASES ARE MORE DIFFICULT TO INVESTIGATE than poltergeist or haunting cases. With poltergeists, we look for clues with the living. With hauntings, we look for an historical connection to the location. But with apparitions, we have the difficulty of gaining information about the ghost who may not even have any connection to the location or to any of the people there.

DETECTION DEVICES

WITH HAUNTINGS there are a variety of environmentally driven devices that can detect anomalies in a location—remember the haunting *is* the location. With apparitions, on the other hand, we need the presence of the entity.

Author trying to detect the Blue Lady, resident ghost of the Moss Beach Distillery.

We can't detect somebody who's not in the room, assuming we have the right tools to begin with.

Presence of an apparition is best determined by human detectors, like witnesses or psychics. Magnetic fields are generally not measurable when the ghost is not present. We have measured moving magnetic fields, proceeding along the path a witness describes as they see the ghost move the same path. The fields might be part of the communication process of the apparition, or unrelated to the apparitional experience.

The connection is not clear. We may yet find a correlation between geomagnetic fields and the interactions of apparitions.

ENERGY

PARAPSYCHOLOGISTS VIEW APPARITIONS AS CONSCIOUSNESS BOUND UP in an energy field or form. What that energy actually is, is subject to debate. The reality may simply be that it's some form of energy our technology cannot detect—yet. This is different from saying it's a new energy. Many forms of energy cannot be detected without the right equipment—like trying to pick up an FM radio signal with an AM radio.

What we detect from the environment as an apparition passes by could be the result of the apparition's energy *interacting* with the energy fields our devices measure. In other words, the detection device picks up the wake of the apparition moving through the environment, like a swimmer feeling the wake of a motor boat moving through the water.

PSYCHICS AND SENSITIVES

IT MAY BE HELPFUL TO USE A HUMAN DETECTOR or a psychic practitioner as a detection "device." Since investigators mainly rely on witnesses' accounts, it can help to bring in a person with ability and training to perceive what is going on paranormally and provide additional information.

I feel good about working with psychics who might produce information to enable me to better understand what's going on. My own investigations with haunting and apparition cases generally involve psychics or sensitives.

BASICS

OST PEOPLE BELIEVE in the possibility of psychic experiences. Of the large number of people who have had such experiences, many have had no opportunity to talk to anyone about them. People call parapsychological research centers with reports of a variety of experiences. Calls and emails range from the need for a simple explanation to a cry for help.

How to Begin

WHEN A CALL COMES IN, the first thing the investigator needs to be is a good listener and a good interviewer. The choice of how to deal with the spontaneous psi experience must be made.

The callers relate the experiences as they see them. Through the interview process we try to get a feeling for how the caller has interpreted the experience. We must ask a variety of questions to get an understanding of what might be happening, both with direct respect to the reported phenomena and what else may be going on in the everyday life of the caller.

A common occurrence is that the reported paranormal experiences are actually window-dressing for some other disturbing event in the caller's life. Therefore, we really need to get the feel of what's happening and determine whether the call is for something that can actually be investigated.

There are three roles the investigator takes on from the moment the call comes in to the finish of the case—detective, magician and counselor.

Detective

THE INTERVIEWING AND DEDUCTIVE SKILLS of a detective are necessary to piece together what's really going on, and who may be causing it, as well as the motive behind the disturbances. Is this deliberate? Stress-related? Or is there some other psychological motivation?

Experiences outside of a controlled environment are spontaneous by nature. They usually happen without any conscious effort on the subject's part to bring them about. To help the person deal with them, we need to know not only *what* has occurred and *how* but also *why*. Learning why something happens not only tells us how to help, it gives us more information on the process behind the appearance of psychic abilities and experiences. With apparitions and poltergeists, we may also have to figure out the *who* of the situation, in order to learn the *how* and the *why*. Then there are the misinterpretations.

Misinterpretations

ONE EXAMPLE OF MISINTERPRETATION CAME UP while I was on a radio show in New York. A caller had reported the odd situation of street lamps going off as he walked by them. While the experience could have been paranormal, it was more probable that it was not. Almost certainly what was happening was that the headlights of passing cars were being reflected into the photoelectric cells of the lamps—the electric eye that automatically turns street lamps on and off as the sun sets and rises. It was perhaps unusual that this happened just as the person was passing that particular light, but only an unusual coincidence, and not paranormal.

MAGICIAN

THE KNOW-HOW OF A MAGICIAN can certainly be helpful if there has been a deliberate, skillful fraud behind the puzzling event. Because magicians use deception to create illusions of magical events, they are quite good at uncovering trickery. While deception is a distinct possibility, it's rare for the fraud to be directed at the investigators. Additionally, there are usually enough cues in the initial phone calls to for experienced ghost hunters to avoid the case.

Fraud is sometimes perpetuated by one family member upon another. The trickster usually drops it when the investigation begins for fear of being caught. So this is not a likely problem by the time the parapsychologist enters the picture.

PERCEPTION

THE INVESTIGATOR SHOULD know something about the psychology of perception— which is one of the fundamental factors in magic—so as to be able to separate misperception of ordinary circumstances from potential paranormal phenomena.

Of course real paranormal phenomena in a case can be misinterpreted, too. The skilled investigator looks at the overall case, but carefully examines each incident both separately and as part of the whole.

From studying the art of magic I gained knowledge that helps me identify fraud in my investigations. Learning the basic principles of magic helped me better understand the psychology of deception and misperception. This comes in handy when trying to understand how people can turn ordinary events into paranormal ones in their minds. The very best magicians have learned how to fool people by understanding how and why that person's perceptions were affected. As magicians learn the psychology of perception and deception, they realize that it is arrogant as to believe that they themselves cannot be fooled.

COUNSELOR

KNOWLEDGE OF PSYCHOLOGY AND BASIC COUNSELING SKILLS are necessary to help the family. People react in fear and confusion to all of the phenomena mentioned in this book. On-site work is particularly helpful in poltergeist cases in helping the family and especially the agent stop the disturbances and work through the stress-inducing circumstances that may have caused the phenomena to begin with. Keep in mind that you can't actually practice therapy or psychology without a license. Parapsychologists such as myself often refer people troubled by weird events to licensed psychotherapists who can handle this part of the situation.

WHY INVESTIGATE?

IT'S IMPORTANT TO UNDERSTAND YOUR OWN MOTIVATIONS for wanting to investigate the paranormal. Too many, would-be ghost hunters could be considered thrill seekers who are not really looking to investigate and understand what's going on, but rather simply out to get a thrill and have an experience. They might want to have an encounter with an apparition, or wish to see things flying around with no apparent motive force. Or most likely, they want to join the throngs of people who are waving around photos of "spirit orbs."

Ask yourself: Are you sincerely interested in understanding the experiences people have, understanding the phenomena, and even though it may turn out to be a normal, though exotic, explanation for ghosts and such? Consider if you are interested in helping people deal with their hauntings and the problems they bring. Answering yes places you in the realm of real paranormal investigators and parapsychologists.

There's nothing wrong with being a thrill seeker, as long as you don't misrepresent yourself to people who may actually need an explanation—and help. In contrast, professionalism demands the investigator dig below the obvious to understand what's going on, and not simply be satisfied with a bunch of unusual photos and weird voices on tape. As an amateur ghost hunter you need to decide upon a direction—towards the thrills or towards understanding. Of course, the path of understanding can also provide a lot of thrills.

CURIOSITY

CURIOSITY ABOUT HUMAN EXPERIENCE puts you into the same realm as the original psychical researchers and most contemporary parapsychological investigators. We paranormal investigators seek to understand why people have these experiences. We struggle to figure out what's really going on and what answers an experience can give to the question of whether there is a life after death.

Paranormal investigators strive to add to humanity's understanding of apparitions, hauntings, and poltergeists and thereby to the understanding of people and consciousness—living and dead. We also seek to help the people having these experiences.

ACTUAL EXPERIENCES

I READ A REPORT OF AN INVESTIGATION conducted by a local ghost-hunting group who conducted an investigation at an estate once used as a sanitarium. There was nothing in their report indicating that people considered the place haunted or had reported ghostly encounters in the recent or more distant past. Why did they go in for an investigation? I can't be sure, but apparently they felt that since it was an abandoned sanitarium, they ought to be able to experience spooky things and get lots of orb photos, too!

There are several problems with this kind of approach. These folks likely went in with the expectation of experiencing something and getting ghost photos. Spooky old buildings can be psychologically suggestive. However, without comparison to the experiences of others in the same place, or comparison to events that happened in the locations history, their experiences have no objective value.

Reports of actual experiences in a particular place—spooky or not—should drive the investigation. Without witness reports, what is there to understand or explain? Why even investigate when there's nothing to investigate?

With witness testimony of experiences, sightings, etc., especially current ones, the investigator has a framework within which to look for normal and paranormal explanations for what has been reported. Without such testimony, there's nothing to investigate so that the so-called investigation is akin to a kind of Halloween haunted house—spooky, thrilling and just a game.

The testimony of people—the human element—points professional paranormal investigators to the locations to investigate, and drives the investigation. It gives us *something* to investigate. And when we encounter no phenomena during an investigation, the witness' testimony—the real ghost stories—keeps us interested.

8

EXPLANATIONS

GHOST HUNTERS MUST SEPARATE THE NORMAL from the paranormal to get to an explanation of what's going on with cases of psychic experience.

I received a call years ago in which an individual who had been having intense headaches and had been seeing things out of the corners of his eyes believed his neighbor—who had "wall-to-wall stereo and other electronic equipment to boost his telepathic powers"—was directing the energy of the equipment at him. The caller also insisted that the neighbor had tapped into his electricity, presumably to help lower the cost of running all that equipment.

I advised the caller to get in touch with the local utilities to investigate the possibility that the neighbor had in fact tapped into his electrical service. I further instructed the caller to say nothing about telepathy—or even the headaches and to avoid mentioning anything paranormal when contacting the utility company.

The utilities folks came out and found: 1) the neighbor was in fact stealing power from the caller and several other neighbors; 2) the neighbor was in fact running wall to wall electrical equipment to apparently protect himself from extraterrestrial influences; and 3) the equipment was giving off a huge amount of electromagnetic energy and low frequency sound—both of which could potentially be responsible for the headaches. The latter could have caused the caller to see things out of the corners of his eyes. So while the caller jumped to paranormal conclusions in his attempt to figure out what was going on—the neighbor looked like the "disturbed" one. He was arrested and fined, by the way.

What this case illustrates is that there may not be a paranormal explanation, and that we can still help in such situations. The mere fact that a researcher took the time to assess the situation and determine that what was going on was not paranormal is more than what others might have done. One woman told me that when she reported her experiences to a local university psychology department, they wanted her to come in for psychological testing to determine if something was wrong with her. Her experience turned out to be a misperception of an ordinary event. Careful assessment is needed of all subjective paranormal experiences if we are to help people understand what is going on in their lives, paranormal or not.

CHECK THE ENVIRONMENT

IN A CASE IN MARTINEZ, CALIFORNIA, a family was renting a relatively new home. The four of them were experiencing dizzy spells in specific spots in the house, intense headaches from time to time, smelled foul odors that had no apparent cause, often felt their hair standing on end, and sighted fireballs mysteriously appearing in and around the house. They thought they were under attack and that the house was haunted. The owner would not let them out of the lease.

They called a local university and were politely told they should seek psychological help. They spoke to a local skeptics group and got the same advice. Something about their claims, notably that there were four witnesses, caused my team to visit the house.

After a short time in the house we all felt dizzy in a couple of spots in the home and even developed headaches when we stood in those spots. We explored the house and considered all the things non-paranormal that could account for what the family was experiencing, and for our own reactions.

The house was directly under lots of power lines. Our electromagnetic field meters measured extremely high fields. The power lines gave off an audible hum, so we knew that we were likely also dealing with low frequency sound.

The house had shifted slightly off its foundation so that the floor was not completely level and some of the doors and window frames were not square. Our perceptual processes try hard to make things neat. Such slight deviations, while generally unnoticed by the conscious mind, can cause people to experience dizziness and headaches.

We detected a lot of static electricity in the house, using a low-tech detector. Waving around a fluorescent light tube through excess static charges will cause it to light up. That accounted for the hair-raising experiences.

If there weren't enough problems, the house was located on the other side of a hill from a landfill. While we were in the house, we noticed a noxious smell—it was methane, likely seeping up through the ground from the landfill. The pockets of methane could catch on fire because of the static electricity. The house was an environmental nightmare, not a paranormal one. One of my team members, familiar with local zoning ordinances, gave the family some good ammunition against the owner that enabled the family to get out of the lease.

Only by thoroughly investigating the location, looking for alternative explanations to "it's haunted" and "they're crazy," that we came to the conclusions that we did. Otherwise, the besieged family was seen as just another flaky or crazy bunch of people.

SOUND WAVES

PARAPSYCHOLOGISTS ARE LOOKING TO UNDERSTAND what apparitions, hauntings and poltergeists are and why they happen. Research is revealing previously-unknown natural explanations, such as that of geomagnetic field influences. Sound may be responsible for some experiences, especially those pesky shadows we see out of the corners of our eyes.

In 1998, Vic Tandy, an expert in computer-assisted learning at Coventry University in England, uncovered another alternative, though unusual, explanation for hauntings—low-frequency sound, or infrasound. Most people think of ultrasonic, or high-frequency sounds, as the only sounds we humans can't hear. We also have a lower threshold of our hearing. Such sounds are infrasonic.

Tests were conducted that revealed the existence of a standing sound wave—a semipermanent sound wave—bouncing around Tandy's lab, where shadows were seen out of the corners of the eyes of a number of people over the years. The sound wave was caused by a fan making the air vibrate at a particu-

No ghosts have been sighted in this Salem, Massachusetts cemetery, but the history is certainly interesting.

lar rate. Once the fan's mounting was altered, the ghost and the sound wave departed.

The standing wave was identified as 19 cycles per second, close to the frequency of infrasound that has apparently been linked to a variety of physiological reactions, from blurring of vision to feelings of unease and fear. NASA research has shown a resonance frequency for the human eyeball of 18 cycles per second—meaning a sympathetic vibration of the eye with low frequency sounds. Since Tandy's report, other researchers have identified sound waves as present in a number of haunting cases.

MISDIRECTION

IN POLTERGEIST CASES, the movement of objects is often noticed out of the corner of the eye, or while an object is already in flight. That people rarely actually see an object take off may be a function of the dynamics of the experience, namely that the attention of all concerned is focused elsewhere when things happen. Just as a magician will misdirect the attention of the audience to a location where nothing is happening so that the "magic" can occur elsewhere, the psychodynamics of a poltergeist case seems to include the same kind of misdirection. If there is a noise in one part of the room—the crashing of a glass against a wall, for example—our attention shifts to that location. This would allow something else to happen in the part of the room where no one is looking at that moment. All in all, it's tough to keep track of all things and all people in a room where PK activity is occurring.

MISINTERPRETATION

MISINTERPRETATION DOES PLAY A ROLE IN OUR CASES. For a few weeks after the 1989 earthquake in San Francisco, I got several phone calls from frantic people thinking they had poltergeists in their homes. Pictures were jumping off the walls, things were falling from shelves, even furniture was being moved slightly. Callers had enough common sense to check if there were aftershocks that could have been responsible. In all cases, there were no coinciding quakes.

Traffic patterns had changed in San Francisco because of the damage caused by the big quake. Construction trucks were driving on streets that before had rarely had such heavy-bodied traffic. The vibrations of the trucks caused the buildings to vibrate, which affected the items within them.

STILL CURIOUS

SKEPTICS AND OTHERS HAVE WONDERED why ghost hunters don't given up investigations, given the number of normal explanations, including newer explanations such as geomagnetic influences and infrasound. They think we ought to be discouraged when we keep finding non-paranormal explanations instead of gaining more understanding of the paranormal. On the contrary, I am energized by new explanations coming out of field and laboratory research in parapsychology.

Our investigations are providing these further pieces in the puzzle of human perception. The more we expand the understanding of our perceptual abilities beyond the traditional senses, the closer we get to understanding psi—which appears to be the perceptual path for interaction with discarnate entities. Some might think I would be discouraged with both the geomagnetic and infrasonic potential explanations, and that there may yet be other more normal, though unusual, explanations for ghosts and hauntings.

AVOID LABELS

INVESTIGATORS MUST CAREFUL TO AVOID LABELING something psychic or paranormal when it may not be. People do misinterpret things and there has been fraud both in and out of the laboratory for a parapsychologist to encounter. Out of the ordinary environmental conditions can cause psi-like experiences and ghostlike sightings. Once we have eliminated as much of the misinterpretation and other ordinary circumstances, we get a better grasp of what may be going on to help the person deal with the experience, whether it turns out to have been normal or paranormal.

Always explore the experience from all sides to see if there might be something normal behind it. But more importantly, look at why the experience was seen as paranormal, how perceptions were altered, and why the experience was interpreted to be paranormal.

Consider whether there are other *psychic* interpretations for apparitional cases and spirit communications. People do pick up information psychically, and sometimes process that information in ways that lead them to believe that the info could only have come from a ghost. This may have to do with the individual's belief system about ghosts and psychic abilities, as well as their willingness, to accept the possibility that they may be psychic.

So, it's important not to jump to conclusions. Look for the normal, even if the normal is out of the ordinary. I will repeat this point in different ways throughout the book because it is so important.

9

INITIAL CALL

WHEN **I** GET A CALL FOR A POTENTIAL CASE, **I must decide if the case is for me. Thrill-seekers hear about** a haunted house and rush over with cameras and other technology to capture something, without considering that there may be nothing paranormal going on at all, or that what's needed is not a ghost photo but some attention to and help for what the people are *experiencing* the phenomenon. Pre-screening is important. Questions need to be answered before we get to the point where we actually go out and investigate.

WHAT TO ASK

ASKING QUESTIONS ABOUT THREE ELEMENTS—logistics, currentness of the phenomena, and availability of witnesses—is particularly important when deciding if you should investigate a reputedly haunted location. An old house, a restaurant, or cemetery might have the *reputation* of being haunted, but without firsthand accounts of experiences, and most importantly without an indication that something *is still happening,* such investigations are generally a waste of time.

LOGISTICS

START WITH AN ASSESSMENT OF THE LOGISTICS. Consider the location of the case and how hard or easy it is to get there and to investigate it. Look at what costs are involved and at how much time it will take. Then consider if this is within your budget of time and money.

Each month, I get calls from all over the country, many worthy of investigation. When I can, I do refer to local investigators, but many locations are far from any appropriate resource. I try to handle those cases by phone, when the cost of travel precludes an on-site investigation. Don't simply shut off the call once you learn it's not local or convenient for you to do the investigation. You may still be able to help the caller over the phone.

CURRENTNESS

HOW CURRENT THE EXPERIENCE is is an important consideration. It is easier to investigate a case when the phenomena is ongoing. Usually, people don't ask for help to stop something unless it still going on. If this is the case, you're closer to the decision to investigate.

If the caller is merely reporting an experience or calling for information, then generally a bit of interviewing, information exchange, and perhaps counseling or referral all that is necessary. Sometimes callers are seeking an explanation for an old experience that still affects them. Without some indication that something is still happening, we are essentially dealing with what police would call a "cold crime scene."

AVAILABLE WITNESSES

ASK ABOUT WITNESSES and what the witnesses have experienced. When there is than one witness the job of determining what is still happening is much easier. Ask

The USS Hornet, a World War II aircraft carrier, now a museum in Alameda, California, and very haunted.

the caller for contact information for the witnesses. Then take time to interview them before determining if the case calls for a visit.

If independent observers have experienced the same things, the situation becomes more interesting to the investigator. There's more potential data. Sometimes, when the investigator does interview witnesses, it turns out that they did not see or experience the same thing as the person who reported the disturbance. With physical disturbances, the objectively ob- served happenings make the decision to investigate easier as compared to an apparitional sighting, which may not have been observed by all witnesses.

CLASSIFY EXPERIENCE

ASK THE CALLER IF ORDINARY EXPLANATIONS have been considered and ruled out. Granted, the average person is not generally aware of all of the possibilities to rule out, but through the pre- screening interview the investigator can usually determine if it's a possible paranormal occurrence or a misinterpreted normal event. If such things have been ruled out, the final determination of the paranormal or psychic status may be delayed pending an in-person look.

When a report is classified as potentially paranormal, the conversation should become an interview, the aim being to determine how firmly the experience can be established as psychic. Sometimes, all that can be determined is that the information is insufficient to definitely exclude the experience from the ranks of the paranormal. The greater part of this determination hinges on how attached a person is to believing that the experience was in fact paranormal.

Next, I try to pin down what *kind* of psychic phenomenon was at work. Was it potentially telepathic or precognitive? Was it clairvoyant? If the figure was seen to appear and disappear, for example, or if an intelligent presence was felt, we would try to determine if the person was seeing an apparition or experiencing a haunting.

The author visiting the control center of the USS Hornet Aircraft Carrier Museum.

INITIAL INTERVIEW QUESTIONS

Answers to the following questions will help you to help
determine whether an investigation is warranted. You objective
is to gain some understanding of the beliefs, background, and
thoughts of the person making the initial contact, which is
generally by phone. The background questions help you to
assess the kind of people involved. Additionally, the questions
will help you probe gently into what the psi disturbance might
be. You will probably want to ask many of these questions of
the others involved if you proceed with an investigation.

1. Describe the occurrences.
2. Where have the occurrences taken place? Address and
    specific locations within the premises, please. Describe
    the premises, please.
3. What are the names and ages of those living or
    working there?
4. What is the relationships of all those in house or
    office to one another?
5. What pets are around?
6. What are the occupations of those in the location?
7. What is the educational background of those in the
    location.
8. How long have you lived or worked there?
9. Did you notice disturbances at any previous addresses?
10. When did the current disturbances begin?
11. What sorts of things went on at the beginning?
12. What did you respond? Feel? What did you do?
13. When was the most recent incident?
14. How frequent are the occurrences ? Is there any
    apparent regularity to their occurrences?
15. Have the disturbances been increasing in frequency and
    severity since they first began?
16. Who are those people directly involved? What did
    they experience?
17. Are there any witnesses from outside the house or
    office? What are their names, occupations, and phone
    numbers. What did they experience, as far as you
    know?
18. Have you noticed a pattern of any kind to these
    disturbances?

19. What ordinary, normal explanations have you considered? Why do you think the events are paranormal?

20. Have you or any of the others involved had my psychic experiences in the past?

21. Have you (or anyone else who witnessed the events) been interested in psychic phenomena? Has family discussed psychic phenomena in the past? If so, in what context?

22. What is your theory as to what may going on? What theories do others have?

23. Have you contacted any "experts"about this? If so, what did they say?

24. What books or articles have you read about psychic phenomena or the occult or supernatural or unsolved mysteries? What is your reaction to them?

25. What films have you seen about psychic phenomena or the occult or supernatural or unsolved mysteries? What did you think of how they portrayed psychic experiences/disturbances?

26. What films, books, TV shows have others involved seen or read?

27. What are your feelings or beliefs regarding psychic phenomena or the spiritual world?

28. What is the family's religious background? Present religious status?

29. Have you ever taken any courses on parapsychology, new age or metaphysical topics, or any self-development or psychic development courses? Which? What was your experience in the course?

30. Have you or any of the others ever been to see a psychic?

31. Has there been any publicity of these events? Has the press found out about what's going on? If so, which members of the media and how can we contact them? If not, can you be sure there won't be any publicity?

32. What would you like done to help you?

33. Would you allow me and some colleagues to do a serious investigation of the occurrences in your home or office?

DETERMINE WHAT IS NEEDED

NEXT, THE INVESTIGATOR DETERMINES HOW TO BEST HELP the person. The interviewing process can achieve this. Simply ask, "What can I do to help you?" Mostly callers are seeking some kind of help—relief from the confusion caused by the experience and from the disruptions of normal activity that the episodes have caused. This may be strongest in the case of poltergeists, since there are physical disturbances affecting the psychology of the home or office and the physical environment and belongings of the people.

For the cold cases, callers typically want to know what the experience was. This is not an easy question to answer because all the facts are generally not available. In such instances, providing general information about psychic experience and apparitions, hauntings, and poltergeists helps. Be honest in telling the caller that it's not likely you can provide a certain explanation to an old experience. Be prepared to provide potential normal explanations.

You must be aware of need on the part of the caller. People usually need an explanation or information on the kind of psychic experience. They may also need a referral to a therapist who is knowledgeable about such experiences, and who can help callers integrate them into their lives.

VALIDATION

SOMETIMES PEOPLE REALLY JUST WANT VALIDATION of the experience—that what they are experiencing is not imagined and doesn't indicate insanity. Often people just want to hear that they're not alone in what they're experiencing and that there are others who report such things.

In the case of apparitions, hauntings, and poltergeists, fear is common, though not necessarily the only reaction. Some people report apparitions to better understand what may be going on, or simply to report an occurrence that the parapsychologist might like to have on file.

Be prepared to refer folks to appropriate psychological resources if it seems needed. Reassure the caller that seeing a counselor to discuss one's fear around a paranormal experience is perfectly normal and quite helpful.

COUNSELING

WHILE MOST OF US ARE NOT PSYCHOLOGISTS, it's important to know that some people will need counseling or more serious psychological help because of the experience and how they've reacted to it. Others may report the phenomena because they are actually psychologically disturbed. Either way, it's important to try to provide a referral to appropriate psychological resources.

By asking targeted questions, you get an understanding of who may be disturbed and having experiences because of their disturbance and who may be disturbed by the phenomena. On the other hand, people may act psychologically disturbed because they have made the wrong conclusions about the bothersome event, such as in the case in which the man believed his neighbor was using technology to beam thoughts at him.

Such assessments are tough to make, and often impossible to determine over the initial phone call. Having other witnesses to contact can be of immense help.

NEVER GO IT ALONE

BE CERTAIN NOT TO BE ON YOUR OWN when conducting most investigations especially in people's homes. It's always good to have others to help with the interviewing, especially interviewing of the witnesses separately. Having other sets of eyes for assessment of the physical location is a big help. Other investigators can help with the thought processes to determine what's going on.

Beyond that, you never know what the actual situation is from a phone interview or how safe it is. For example, you could walk into a domestically volatile situation, or a situation with a disturbed person. There is little to fear from the phenomena, but living beings are another thing. In other words, the only real physical danger your face in cases can come from the people involved, rather than the ghosts. Ghosts don't carry guns and knives, but I've encountered disturbed individuals on cases who were carrying both.

The safety issue is rarely a concern when investigating public haunts. However, bringing along a couple of assistants to help with observation and assessment is generally advisable.

AVOID PUBLICITY AND DEBUNKERS

OFTEN PEOPLE CALL SIMPLY FOR CURIOSITY'S SAKE. I've had a number of excellent cases that developed out of calls where the callers wanted a better understanding of what was happening to them, and were experiencing little or no fear.

Another motive is more mercenary. On occasion, calls come in from people expecting me to help them validate their experience so they can sell the story to TV or movie producers. They want an investigation for the excitement of sharing what's going on with the world. These folks are often seeking publicity.

Often these more self-serving motives signal a situation that could get out of hand and cause inaccurate information to get out—and damage your reputation. The desire for publicity can also be an indication of potential fraud.

On the other hand, publicity can be fine if it's a public place such as a restaurant, bar, hotel, or museum. Just be sure that the issues of logistics, currentness, and witnesses have been resolved. It is important that you have control over the investigation and are free to state that nothing is happening if this is your conclusion. Some of my best cases involved public locations with lots of publicity. The money a production company brings to the table can overcome many logistical blocks.

A final motive is the desire to fool you, the investigator. Some skeptics may try to set you up for embarrassment with a false case. I've avoided this trap by asking the right questions directed at the issues discussed earlier in this chapter when pre-screening. If I am at all suspicious that the case is a setup, I check my suspicions with skeptics I know. I've made it a point to get to know some of the local vocal skeptics. While many who call themselves skeptics are actually disbelievers and debunkers, there are usually a few reasonable people in every skeptics group. I've gotten to know some of these people and expressed respect for their agnostic viewpoint. From time to time I call on some of these people to give me "a second opinion" when I have suspicions of trickery.

Armed with the information from the call, it helps to really think through alternative explanations and plan out your investigation. But keep in mind that things are often *not* what you first think they are.

OTHER CONSIDERATIONS

SOME PEOPLE FEEL THEIR EXPERIENCES ARE UNIQUE and expect investigators to jump at the chance to do a bit of psi testing. Some people do have unique experiences which may be recurring, and they may have abilities that prove to be under some degree of control. But parapsychological centers are not equipped to do the kinds of massive testing necessary to test everyone who reports psychic experiences.

Ghost hunters are interested in hearing about people's experiences and want to help people deal with them and want to understand what's going on with them. But there has to be something that can be investigated to warrant an investigation.

As you can see, many factors go into the decision to investigate. As we explore methods of ghost hunting, I'll take you a bit more into how we decide what's really going on and what to do about it.

10

ASSESSING THE CASE

OU'VE PRE-SCREENED THE CALL and decided to investigate the case. It is useful to have the caller and other witnesses reconstruct a chronology of what *has* happened. Also it is important that witnesses keep track of any new events.

The best cases are ones in which frequent events are reported. These cases hold the hope that investigators will get a chance to experience the phenomena. When the events are spread far apart and there is no pattern for when they occur, it is unlikely that the phenomena will occur when investigators are at the site.

When there has been an observed pattern to the events, a stakeout can be arranged for an attempt to observe the reported phenomena. This is the ideal which rarely presents itself since in real-life situations, most people have not thought to look for common factors and have not noticed a pattern, unless it was very obvious.

INITIAL ASSESSMENT

THE FIRST STEP IS TO ASSESS THE UP-FRONT INFORMATION to formulate an initial theory of what might be going on. Weighing the likelihood that it may be an apparition, haunting, or poltergeist case rather than one of the other phenomena should drive preparation for the investigation. The investigator must always keep in mind that this is a "theory" and not be locked into an initial assessment. Doing so separates the ghost hunter from the merely curious, so always be aware of your own preconceptions and biases.

GATHER INFORMATION

INTERVIEW ALL PARTIES INVOLVED TO GET A FULL PICTURE of what may be going on before. There can be conflicting details of the events reported by the various people involved, which adds to the difficulty of making an initial assessment.

Ask who the witnesses have spoken with about the experience. Find out what they were told by other investigators, psychics, or clerics they may have contacted. Ask what family members and friends have told them. You may have to do damage control if well-meaning friends and so-called experts have provided bad information, which happens more often than we'd like.

It is often the case that other experts have provided good information that the caller can't accept and is calling you to get an explanation he or she can believe. You must decide if an investigation is warranted and worth your time, if they are not going to listen to you.

Visit the location to look for the normal explanations based on the environment. Match this to the events detailed by each of the witnesses and to the overall context of the case. Interview at the location as many people as possible who were involved, so as to observe their behavior in that location. You may notice differences in their stories *because* they are in the location. Ask many questions and keep coming up with new ones to ask.

BE SKEPTICAL

TO BE A GOOD INVESTIGATOR remember to be an open-minded skeptic. I stress the necessity to look for normal physical and psychological causal factors and to not jump to the conclusion of "Yep, that's paranormal, all right." Not only may you be wrong in your conclusion, but most often the people involved are seeking reassurance that they are not going crazy and that the experiences are normal.

People do misinterpret normal events as paranormal ones and group other unusual, though normal, events in with the initial experiences—even though the other incidents are totally unrelated to the original phenomena.

WITHHOLD JUDGMENT

BE CAREFUL TO NOT DRAW CONCLUSIONS as to what kind of paranormal experience this may be over the initial phone calls . You may decide not to even make such conclusions on the first visit, unless things are quite clear. Things are rarely "just a ghost." Be careful about stating your ongoing flow of theories about the phenomena in a committed-sounding manner.

GIVE INFORMATION

PROVIDE THE PEOPLE INVOLVED WITH GENERAL INFORMATION about psychic phenomena. Usually when people read what parapsychologists have learned about the phenomena, there is a dramatic lessening of fear—often accompanied by an increase in curiosity.

KEEP A LOG

INSTRUCT WITNESSES TO KEEP CLOSE TABS ON THEIR EXPERIENCES, especially any new events. Advise them to keep a journal of their experiences, either written or on audio

tape. They should make an account of any new experience as immediately as possible, without an assessment
or interpretations of what was experienced. Tell them to
note the full details of the experience, including their
position in the location along with the positions of
everything and everyone else present. They should
record a description of anything unusual that they may
see, such as an apparitional sighting. If any objects
move this should be described in the journal. Advise
clients to always describe how they feel before, during,
and after the experience. Tell them to record accounts
from all others in the location.

There may be some meaning to why the experience
happened at that point in time, symbolic or otherwise.
The client's own interpretation, once somewhat removed
in time from the experience, often sheds some light on
this. To get at these possibilities, instruct the client to
go back over that data at a later time and to jot down
interpretations and reactions of what went on. This
follow up data collection should include interpretations
of any others who were around.

Your encouragement is important in
motivating clients to keep good journals. Tell the client to alert you to
any new events so that you can
visit to observe as soon after
a report as possible.

11

INTERVIEWING
WITNESSES

OUR GHOST HUNTING TOOLS INCLUDE YOUR ABILITY to be an objective observer, your knowledge of possibilities for the reported experience, both normal and paranormal— and your interviewing skills. Your ability to pull information from witnesses is the best tool you have in uncovering what's really going on—and why.

Information you gather from witnesses is the most important data you have from which to piece together an understanding of what's going on. It's also the most interesting, too. Through the information you get during the interview process you'll develop a picture of what's been happening on both paranormal and normal levels. You may need to ask tough personal questions that cause emotional discomfort and have to push for those answers. Witnesses may be resistant. With good interviewing skills you can get the answers you need to properly assess the situation.

Interview all parties concerned. Take each witness's testimony separately. Also interview each witness when all witnesses are together in a group. More than one interview of each witness should take place to see if the details are consistent over time. It

The USS Hornet has had dozens of apparition sightings since docked in Alameda, California in 1995.

also gives you an opportunity to ask questions about details of the event you didn't have in the first interview.

BE DISCERNING AND PROBE

THE MIND IS CAPABLE OF MISINTERPRETATION. Perceptions of a given situation can be altered. Some people make things up, consciously or unconsciously. People forget minor details and tend to remember their interpretations more easily than what actually happened. Some features of the experience may have been more attention-grabbing than others and overshadow what is remembered. Often pieces are left out because they were hidden from the perceptions of the people who had the experience. The initial perception of events is often incomplete so it is important to probe for possible conditions other than those originally described.

Cases with multiple witnesses generally work a bit better because the recollections and perceptions of each witness provide a slightly different piece to the puzzle. Testimony may be contradictory. Perhaps everyone did not experience the paranormal event or perhaps what was experienced was not paranormal. Look for a consensus of what happened.

The witnesses may have discussed their experiences among themselves before you were able to talk to them separately. In the process they may have contaminated each other's stories, and changed their original picture of what happened. As often happens, one of the witnesses was more persuasive than the others so that you only have the story of that one witness told by several, and not a general consensus.

People tend to remember only those things that fit their personal view of the way things work in the world, so that without realizing it, they have selectively remembered the things fit with their story. A related problem is that witnesses can make up details without realizing it. Making up details could be a sign of fraud, but it's more likely that the witness was unconsciously filling in the blanks.

Another thing to watch for is the tendency of witnesses to repeat more often or embellish those details that seem to be of more interest to you.

RECREATE THE EVENT

A RECREATION OF EVENTS MAY HELP TO JOG PEOPLE'S memory. Walk everyone through where they were and what they were doing when the events happened. Witnesses may remember something not reported before by carefully going over what happened from start to finish.

A reconstruction of events can uncover perceptual problems. For example, unusual lights or figures may actually have been reflections that disappear when viewed from other angles. The physical locale itself may suggest certain information to those in it. A spooky old house, for example, may suggest to visitors the idea of ghosts so that any normal creaking noises produced by the house or any dark shadows send visitors running. As witnesses reconstruct the experience, you can point out such elements. It is just as important to investigate what was *not* reported as it is to question what was.

Coincidences

REPORTED EVENTS MAY BE COINCIDENCES that have been given extra meaning by witnesses. For this reason it's important to dig deeply into any case, for the facts behind what is happening to understand why the people are having this experience at this point in time. Look for patterns in the events that are more than just coincidental.

Expectations

SUGGESTIBILITY CAN BE ANOTHER PROBLEM. When told a place has a ghost or is haunted, witnesses tend to give into imagination and fears. Find out who knew what, and when. Check what each witness knew about the event and who may have talked with them about it. But don't be too quick to dismiss a situation, such as when the observer knew of the dead person, since apparitions are often of deceased relatives who witnesses would naturally have known. Offset suggestibility by looking for that display of intent and intelligence in the behavior of the ghost.

Also consider that a real paranormal event, depending on the reaction to it, may cause the witnesses to become sensitive to sounds and movements they normally don't notice. Seeing a ghost may have led witnesses to assume house-settling noises are also caused by the ghost, for example.

VISIT THE SITE

CHECK THE PHYSICAL LOCATION CAREFULLY to see if you observe other factors that may have had something to do with what was reported. It may help to check records of local weather patterns and earth movements, as well as traffic patterns for any potentially disturbing outside influence on the location.

UNCOVER BELIEFS

PROBE TO UNCOVER THE BELIEFS of the witnesses. Find out their ideas about the occult and supernatural. Do they read tabloids and take their stories seriously? Probe into the impact from films and television on their beliefs. Ask about previous psychic experiences

The forecastle area at the bow of the USS Hornet Aircraft Carrier. One of the real paranormal hot spots of the ship.

they may have had. Ask about what their friends believe about the paranormal. Inquire about what books they may have been read on these topics. Ask about their religious beliefs and practices and probe how religion plays into their views about psychic phenomena.

This information can help you understand how susceptible the witnesses are to suggestion and mistakenly classifying the normal as paranormal or supernatural. It will help you to talk with them about their experiences and in determining how to best counsel them to deal with the experiences.

For example, you will need to take more care with a person who assumes all psychic experiences are the result of outside forces, whether demonic or heavenly. A believer in the entity idea might resist the idea that the poltergeist is caused by a living mind. By comparison, someone who hasn't yet formed an opinion on such things or who has been exposed to some of the more occult ideas would probably be more accepting of the human causes of poltergeists. Religious beliefs, especially when they includes demons and the like, can make things difficult because your information and advice conflict with those beliefs, there may be little or no acceptance of what you have to say.

Pathology

INVESTIGATORS MUST BE CAREFUL TO PROBE into the psychological state of the witnesses to determine if the experiences could be due to psychopathology or other psychological issues. Unfortunately, a psychological component is fairly common. People call asking for help with "telepathic attacks" by ghostly hallucinations. These cases are difficult to deal with because

Catwalk in the USS Hornet's forecastle, site of several ghost sightings.

the people tend to resist any consideration of a psychological or brain-related cause of the experience.

Another consider is physiological problems. Their symptoms may have been misinterpreted to be caused by something paranormal. I often refer people to medical doctors when their description of a psychic attack includes pains and other physical symptoms.

Don't get into psychological and physiological treatments unless you're a trained psychotherapist or M.D. Refer people with these issues to expert practitioners. On the other hand, realize that jumping to conclusions about a witness's psychological state can be very wrong.

PSYCHOLOGICAL DYNAMICS

THE PSYCHOLOGY AND HUMAN RELATIONSHIPS in all psychic experience can affect the experiences and the reasons behind them. In poltergeist cases, we must look at interpersonal relationships, as well as stressors such as job, school, and so forth. It can be helpful to have the members of the family or group involved go through psychological testing, including personality type, suggestibility, and other indicators we use to correlate with psychic ability.

In apparition cases, we consider the psychology that the apparition represents. The reason why the apparition is around seems to have much to do with the discarnate individual's personality. Often, dealing with the apparition requires the investigator to counsel the ghost. Fortunately, the laws regarding doing therapy without a license don't cover apparitions as clients.

Making Recordings

REMEMBER THIS IMPORTANT POINT: Pay attention to the motivational and psychological aspects of the situation to learn the *why* of the experiences. This is sometimes difficult for the outside observer. In the case of poltergeist experiences, make especially careful observations of the interrelationships of the people involved. Sometime it makes sense to record the family members interacting normally in the home or other site of the disturbances.

Monitoring of the situation—with a tape recorder and still camera, with video cameras, or with other electronic monitoring devices—can add to verbal reports and provide a record of what is said. It helps to be in the right place at the right time, so look for potential patterns in the experiences to determine when and where to monitor. This is where the data in witnesses' journals can help. All recording devices should be unobtrusive and the investigator should try to blend into the background.

BE ALERT TO YOUR BIASES

FROM MY BACKGROUND IN MAGIC AND MENTALISM I have developed an alternate framework that enables me to understand how normal events might be seen as paranormal ones. Psychology of perception is important to both the magician and to the parapsychologist. Magicians put these principles into action to create the illusion of the paranormal—to make magic. Parapsychologists, on the other hand, use these principles to expose illusions and get to what really occurred.

Investigators need to constantly assess their own biases. We all have a tendency to categorize experiences we learn about in certain ways before really looking deeply at what's going on. As investigators, we must examine and be guarded against our own biases, since they can affect how questions are asked, how answers are received, and how the accounts are integrated and interpreted

Your questions influence witness recall and reconstructions of events. What you show interest in may encourage a witness to embellish. Probe testimony to get to the core of what may be going on and to ensure the quality of your field research. When writing up or reporting an investigation, be careful to report the objective assessment of the situation, and note your own subjective reactions or interpretations as such.

WHOLE AND SEPARATE

CONSIDER NOT ONLY THE ISSUE OF THE OVERALL CASE being paranormal, but also if the individual events are normal or paranormal. Be very careful to break down the case into component parts, into those individual events, to make your assessment. You are then in a position to better separate the normal from the paranormal events, as well as to better determine which paranormal events relate to one another.

Assessment of the components of the case and how they fit into the whole enables you to explain the non-paranormal events. Generally you will only be able to give an educated guess about what the original event *might have been*. Nonetheless, you still play a vital role in helping witnesses by explaining to them the causes behind the subsequent observations and experiences.

Maintain Confidentiality

MOST PEOPLE WHO CALL FOR HELP OUT OF FEAR don't even want their neighbors to know what's going on, let alone the rest of the world. Maintaining confidentiality— the specifics of who the people are and where they live—is crucial to the ethical behavior of an investigator.

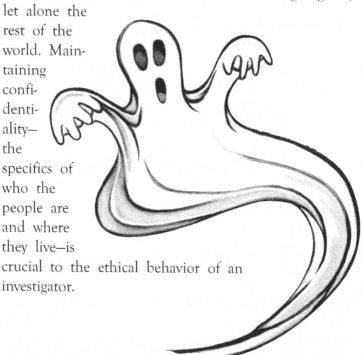

12

FRAUD

ECEPTION IS ALWAYS A POSSIBILITY. **The caller may have made up or greatly enhanced the story. Some people go so** far as to actually stage the occurrences, such as rigging things to fall from the wall. Uncovering this sort of deception can be quite difficult. Don't assume that this sort of fraud is perpetrated solely on the investigators and the press. Actually, fraud happens most often in ghost-related cases because one family member has *issues* with another.

Motives

MOST OF THE TIME, THE MOTIVES FOR FRAUD ARISE out of relationship issues within the family. Sometimes motives have psychological roots. Referral to individual and/or family counseling is the best way to handle these cases.

When deception involves only one person, it may be to gain attention. A lonely woman, for example, may convince herself that there really is a ghost in her house as a way of asking for attention. Single witness cases can be among the most difficult to assess because, not only may there be no physical indicator that anything has happened or is still happening, but there's usually no corroboration for the story.

In a family setting, one member of the family may feel unseen, for example, and make up a story about a ghost or demon to become the center of attention. If the family is prone to explaining things in terms of religion or the paranormal they may unwittingly buy into and support the story's development by having their own ghostly experiences themselves. In such cases the people actually believe that something is happening in their home, and the suggestion affects them in such a way as to cause them to perceive something disturbing themselves.

When there are suspicious signs, I consider possible motives and check the reliability and sincerity of testimony. If the experience was *real* to the witness, then fraud is generally ruled out. On the other hand, although unusual, a hoaxer may use various means to fool others into thinking that they experienced an apparitional sighting. Fraudulent spiritual mediums are well-known to have used a range of methods to fool their clients into believing that they can communicate with spirits of the dead. In this example, the experiences are real to the people participating in the séance, called sitters, but fraudulent deception is caused by one individual—the medium.

UNCONSCIOUS TRICKERY

TRICKERY CAN BE *UNCONSCIOUSLY* PRODUCED by one or more persons in the environment. Given the existence of disorders like kleptomania—where a person can not resist the urge to take things and may not even be aware of having done so—anything is possible. Should you encounter a case involving unconscious fraud, it's generally best to be tactful in your explanation.

IMITATIVE FRAUD

PURPOSEFUL FRAUD IS THE INTENT TO DECEIVE right from the start. There is also what the late parapsychologist W. Edward Cox called "imitative fraud," in which someone in the environment—such as a poltergeist agent who is generally unaware of causing the phenomena—adds in a few deliberate deceptive actions in imitation of the phenomena already witnessed. Given that any events similar to the actual phenomena will be blamed on the poltergeist, the deliberate imitative deception may provide a *conscious* tension release.

RSPK phenomena *are* present in the imitative case, whereas with purposeful fraud the deceiver used trickery right from the start. Either way, the investigator must keep close tabs on everyone to watch for fraud.

PROFIT MOTIVE

HOAXERS OFTEN HAVE MERCENARY MOTIVES. I've gotten numerous calls over the years from people who tell me a little of their story and then quickly turn to asking how much money they might make from it. I respond by saying that asking about making money from such events raises red flags of fraud. Those who don't immediately hang up rarely want an indepth investigation, but seem after just an *opinion* of what *might* be happening, which raises more red flags. I know of such discussions of possibilities that were misused as the "victims" tried to get media attention. I can almost hear them now, saying, "I spoke to Loyd Auerbach—that ghost hunter— and he said it is a ghost!"

I am generally suspicious of cases that come through the media because some folks may hope to get a movie deal or a book contract. However, I do get many legitimate cases via television and radio shows as well as newspapers because the media is often the only source people have to ask for a referral to get help. In fact, some of my best cases have come via media channels. It's wise to be skeptical—but also be fair.

WATCH WITNESSES

CASES WITH PHYSICAL PHENOMENA have the inherent problem that no one investigator or camera can see all points of a room at all times. It is helpful to keep track of the people involved rather than trying to watch all the objects. Objects can be rigged to move, of course, so it is wise to thoroughly check all the objects in the setting.

Witnesses suspected of staging fraudulent effects should be watched for movements that might relate to the movement of objects. For example, movement of a hand near a lamp just before it fell to the floor may mean that the person tugged the lamp cord when you momentarily turned your attention away.

Being vigilant is imperative in such cases. Even when you've set up controls to guard against fraud-producing activity, a determined person can find new ways to deceive. Investigators must constantly update their controls.

13

PSYCHICS

HE QUESTION INVARIABLY COMES UP **when work-ing with self-proclaimed psychics—how do you know how psychic they are? There's no easy** answer to this question, especially considering the range of people who claim to have psychic abilities.

Continuum of Usefulness

AT ONE END OF THE CONTINUUM are phonies, frauds, and con artists, at the other end are genuinely talented psychics. It is fairly easy to convince many people that one is psychic. Some, who do it for entertainment, can be quite good observers and can be helpful in an investigation. Others, however, may be focused only on money, fame, and power.

Big Egos

SELF-CENTERED PSYCHICS, regardless of ability level, tend to be ineffective in investigative cases. While they may talk a good talk about what they're "getting," they tend to have a vested interest in being "right." Sometimes these prima donna-types even contradict witnesses, especially when they have not been given the background of the case. Many talk of curses and black auras and negative energies, which they can usually "get rid of" for a price. Stay away—far away—from these people.

SELF DECEPTION

SELF-DECEIVING PSYCHICS ARE IN THE MIDDLE of the continuum. These are people who may have some psychic ability, but are generally excellent observers. Because their perceptions are insightful, others have convinced them that they are psychic. Such people can be useful to an investigation because they may they may be able to notice things at the location or about the specifics of a case no one else might have noticed. They often determine the normal explanations for what people thought were paranormal occurrences. Be wary, however, of those who are ego-invested and need your approval and pronouncement that they are indeed psychic.

GENUINE PSYCHICS

GENUINE PSYCHICS ARE PEOPLE who have *noticed* their psi and paid more attention to it, therefore bringing it more into their conscious minds. These folks can

The author with paranormalist Uri Geller and the late Japanese psychic Aiko Gibo.

Author with psychic Annette Martin at the Moss Beach Distillery.

often pick up the specific imprints responsible for hauntings, or the stress coming off the poltergeist agents, or even see or sense apparitions. Unfortunately, they can bring their own conceptual or egocentric baggage to a case.

Too many genuine psychics have not been trained to detect the differences between apparitions and hauntings, and poltergeists. Some of them may have religious beliefs that color how they assess what they pick up. Actually, psychics tend to be more trouble than they're worth when they are unable to step back from their perceptions, in response to an investigator's questions. There's often an ego or self-esteem issue, so that they feel the need to prove their psychic-ness to others. Others may come to the case with an "I'm so special" attitude.

Ultimately, it doesn't matter how psychic someone is if you can't work with them, or if they cause more harm than help, or if they insist on being the center of attention, or they must be "right," or if they simply "don't play well with others."

WORKING WITH PSYCHICS

I OFTEN WORK WITH PSYCHICS. I prefer professionals who I've tested in earlier cases. Occasionally I will bring in a person I've casually met who seem *sensitive* to the phenomena that I encounter in cases. In selecting a psychic, I consider two main issues. First, are they providing value and additional information in the cases? Second, do they work well with the investigators and the witnesses?

I use psychics in the same way I use detectors. I let them tell me what they perceive in the moment and where that something is. Then I use environmental detectors to see if any pick up anything anomalous in the same spots. I check the psychic's perceptions against those of the witnesses in that moment. If the detection device or a witness should pick something up, I call the psychic over to scan the area. As a rule of thumb, let your detectors—the technological devices, the witnesses, or the psychics—point out the anomalies, then use the others to back them up.

Psychic Neva Turnock getting a sense of the USS Hornet.

I also work with non-psychics. I have brought in people who have had psychic experiences and those who have not had such experience to work a field experiment, such as the descriptive list of adjectives, a technique explained in a later chapter.

SELECTING PSYCHICS

I USUALLY FIND PSYCHICS BY WORD OF MOUTH—mostly through other investigators. I work with those willing to volunteer their time on a couple of cases to give me a chance to assess their value. I do not assess them by having them do a reading for me. That's too personal and too easy for phonies to manipulate. Also, it's important to realize that a genuine psychic reader may not be particularly good on an actual investigation.

Psychics come with their own beliefs. Investigators are wise to explore what they believe about apparitions, hauntings, and poltergeists before utilizing their commentary.

TOOLS FOR PSYCHICS

SOMETIMES A PSYCHIC WILL USE A TOOL, such as Tarot cards, rune stones, or Ouija Board, as an enhancement or focal point. On the one hand, many psychics use enhancement tools because they have little faith in their own abilities. Others seek to attribute outcomes—good or bad—to the cards, stones, or board, so that they don't have to take any blame for wrong information.

14

TECHNOLOGY

ANY GHOST HUNTING GROUPS **have become enamored with technology. Like other investigators, I've found** that technology *can* be useful in detecting anomalous energies, but a reliance on it can also be misleading— a bad idea when trying to understand what is or is not going on. Technological devices used in ghost hunting usually have been developed for other purposes, such as to identify certain environmental conditions. None are proven to actually detect ghosts or other psychic phenomena.

Many in the "gizmo school" of ghost hunting believe that using technological devices means they must be doing "real" science. Yes, technology comes from the application of science, but using it hardly means one is doing scientific research and investigation. A chimpanzee can learn to use a camera or EMF meter, but that doesn't mean the chimp is being scientific. Using the scientific method to determine what is and is not detected by such devices is doing science. Looking for an explanation of what's being detected is doing science.

DEFINED BY EXPERIENCE

TECHNOLOGICAL DEVICES ARE FUN AND OFTEN USEFUL, but the emphasis in any investigation must be placed on the *human experience*. Psychic abilities and experiences are defined by the context of interactions of the human mind. Apparitions are defined by their interaction with witnesses. Hauntings are defined by the perceptions of witnesses. Poltergeists are defined by living people observing and affecting the environment with their minds.

In other words, the phenomena investigated by parapsychologists are defined *by people* and depend on the witnesses having experiences or and the people who may be causing the phenomena and not on some technology designed for other purposes.

WHAT TECH DETECTS

JUST AS INVESTIGATORS MUST CHECK THE PERCEPTIONS of a witness for non-paranormal explanations, we must always consider non-paranormal causes for anomalies such as unusual images on photos, unusually high magnetic fields, strange temperature variations, and so on. Keep in mind that none of the devices were designed to detect ghosts or hauntings or even consciousness. The anomalies, while they might be related to apparitions, hauntings, poltergeists, and other psychic "energy"—if that's even the right word—could also be related to unknown or unrecognized other phenomena.

Haunting phenomena are environmental in nature and often reoccur in patterns. Investigators using magnetometers in haunting cases have found correlations between unusual magnetic fields and the specific locations people experience the phenomena. The magnetic fields are on different frequencies, including the geomagnetic range, and have no apparent source. The view among many parapsychologists is that some form of magnetic-related field in the environment records events and that humans have the ability to play back these events. However, when using a magnetometer or EMF meter or other devices that might pick up the magnetic fields put out by electronic devices and wiring, you may have to turn off the power in the building to get an accurate reading. Furthermore, water flowing through pipes can sometimes create enough of an energy field to be detectable.

Is Anybody There?

READINGS RARELY CHANGE LOCATION IN HAUNTINGS, which makes sense since it's the environment that provides the anomalous information. So an unusual reading means only that something unusual is happening in the environment. A human perception of something is required to connect the reading to a haunting.

Author using a magnetometer at the Moss Beach Distillery.

Whether or not
something can be
detected in apparition
cases is dependent on
the ghost being *present
when the sensors are used.*
Since apparitions have
free will like living
folks, there's little we
can do to detect one
if the ghost doesn't
feel like coming
around. Because an
apparition is a form of

*The author checking a spot for
activity with a meter as psychic
Kathy Reardon looks on.*

consciousness, and science is undecided as to whether
consciousness actually exists in the body—let alone after
death and outside the body—using technological devices
in such cases doesn't prove anything to science.

Investigators have found instances when people have
experienced an apparition at the same time various
detectors have picked up on something anomalous.
Human experience defines a phenomenon as an apparition. An anomalous readings by a device *confirms* that
something is occuring in the environment that seems to
correlate to the human experience.

LIMITATIONS

A SINGLE READING ON A DETECTION DEVICE must be
considered with caution. Without a correlation to
something else the reading has little meaning. At the
very least someone should have a perception of the
ghost or the spot should have a history of reported
paranormal phenomena or experiences.

Always beware of the limitations of the equipment you use and how false readings might be

produced. By false, I mean that the readings are otherwise explainable and *not* actually paranormally connected when examined closely. Do not rely on technology to tell you a place is haunted or a ghost is present. People make incorrect assumptions about places and their evidence. People love to believe graveyards are haunted, for example, but in reality, ghost sightings in cemeteries are extremely rare. Just because a body's buried somewhere doesn't make the place haunted. Don't make similar assumptions abut technology.

ENVIRONMENTAL ANOMALIES

THE APPROPRIATE USE OF TECHNOLOGY is to establish correlations between anomalous human experience, environmental anomalies and our models of what apparitions and hauntings are. There is some evidence that certain technological devices can help us better understand what's going on when someone sees a ghost.

Are the devices detecting apparitions or hauntings? Perhaps. We can say with certainty that in some cases anomalies are detected in the environment that do correlate with people's experiences. Based on these apparent correlations we speculate that an apparition causes these anomalies—but we can't be certain. From those speculations we draw hypotheses that whatever caused the anomalies also caused people to have haunting and apparitional experiences, but we can't be certain. Our hypotheses must be tested—and that's, in part, what ghost hunting is about—defining the limits of our perceptions.

It will take a lot more research with all sorts of technologies, including computers that can take in the readings and correlate them statistically, before we will be able to point a gizmo at a spot, get a reading, and shout, "We got one!" Unfortunately, it will take a lot of money to do that research—funds which most researchers don't have.

The plus to the increasing use of technology in paranormal investigations is that it provides more opportunities to collect data about the connection between the environment and human experiences. Technology is useful only when the equipment is used properly, when data from the device is recorded and correlated with experiential data.

POLTERGEIST EXCEPTION

APPLICATION OF DETECTION TECHNOLOGY in poltergeist cases hasn't shown to be very helpful. Poltergeist cases generally involve a living person at the root of it all. While I have not had an opportunity to use a geomagnetometer in a poltergeist cases—as of yet the other devices I've used have detected nothing, even when something in the room was actually in motion. Motion detectors are useless when people are in a room, and rarely does anythng happen when the poltergeist agent is out of the room.

The best detection devices in poltergeist cases are video cameras. Make sure the whole room is within the range of the cameras, as poltergeist phenomena has a wonderfully frustrating capacity for happening *behind* the cameras.

MALFUNCTIONING EQUIPMENT

THERE IS A LAST IMPORTANT PIECE OF ADVICE when it comes to the use of technology—whether high- or low-tech. Beware of malfunctioning equipment and drained batteries. While they seem to indicate that something paranormal is happening—you're stuck without a way to record it.

I've been on many cases when our devices have malfunctioned. An apparent drained battery is the most common problem. I've seen fully charged batteries drain within minutes of walking into some locations. Audio and video recording devices that were tested and working produced blank tapes or were full of recorded static. TV crews working with us on some cases have endured continual problems with battery drainage. Interestingly enough, by simply walking the equipment outside the building the batteries recharge and malfunctioning equipment works again.

"Wow! This is incredible!" It is a strong indication that *something* anomalous is happening in the environment. The important lesson is that in some very active cases, relying on technology *only* can be a very big mistake: What do you do when the tech stops working? This brings us full circle and back to the experiences of living people. If you wish to detect a ghost, invest more time in interviewing witnesses and in making observations than in taking readings. Remember, tech can fail. In any event, a good ghost story is more exciting than a single high reading.

Ouija Boards

LET ME SAY A FEW WORDS ABOUT OUIJA BOARDS. Many people try to use the boards to try to contact spirits. I don't use Ouija Boards in cases, but not for the reason you may think.

There is *nothing* inherently evil or demonic about Ouija Boards. They are simply a patented form of a method used during the latter 19th Century to ostensibly communicate with spirits. People wishing to contact spirits would lay out cards with the alphabet and numbers on them in a circle on a table. An overturned glass would be placed in the center, and each sitter around the table would place a finger on the glass. A question would be asked and the glass would move from card to card spelling out answers.

There was never any real evidence that *spirits* directed the glass. Actually, the glass and the Ouija Board's pointer, called a *planchette*, moves as a result of a phenomenon called the ideomotor response.

Using a pendulum is similar. The pendulum is a string or chain with a weight, like a ring or crystal, suspended from it. The pendulum is held loosely by the string so that it can swing freely. A question is asked while concentrating on the dangling ring. Amazingly, it usually moves—bank and forth for "Yes!", or up-and-down for "No!" if those are the directions you assigned for yes and no. The ideomotor response is operating in both cases—with the Ouija Board and with the pendulum. The answer is a result of unconsciously driven minor muscle movements and not spirits of dead people. The subconscious mind makes the things move—not spirits

Ouija Boards have never been shown to tap into spiritual sources. But there is much to suggest that it taps the subconscious mind of the users who may have access to otherworldy information via their own psychic abilities.

Any danger in using Ouija Boards is in taking the "communications" literally. Ouija Board users should take the information they receive the way they would take a dream. Both hold meaning which is open to interpretation.

When two or three people have fingers on the planchette, it's next to impossible to know whose subconscious is putting out the communication. You probably

Classic Ouija Board

wouldn't take your own unconsciously-derived communications literally, so you should *definitely not* take advice from someone else's unconscious communicated through an Ouija Board.

EASILY MANIPULATED

THERE'S ALWAYS A POSSIBILITY THAT SOMEONE working the board with you is *purposely* moving the planchette to particular letters and numbers. This is especially true when college students, teens, and kids are using the boards for entertainment.

If you keep two things in mind Ouija Boards will not be a concern: First, the Ouija Board taps the subconscious, not the spiritual. Second, Ouija Board are generally sold in toy stores and game shops. Don't take "answers" from a board any more seriously than any other toy or game you might play with, and you'll never have a problem with it.

There are many occult detection devices, like crystal balls and the tarot.

15

ENVIRONMENTAL SENSORS

F YOU ELECT TO USE TECHNICAL EQUIPMENT, there is an array of detection devices available. Modern ghost hunters can choose among magnetic field detectors, thermometers, video and still cameras, and other environmental sensors.

MAGNETOMETERS

I HAVE FOUND THE MOST USEFUL DEVICES are the magnetic field detectors—or magnetometers. These meters can work on different frequencies and are capable of detecting different kinds of magnetic fields, so it helps to have more than one type.

TriField Meter

THE MOST COMMONLY USED MAGNETOMETER is the TriField Meter, so called because it can measure three types of fields—magnetic, electric, and radio/microwave. They are most useful in the magnetic mode. The basic meters are designed to detect energy fields given off by technology. So when taking a reading during an investigation you may have to shut off the power to make sure you're not getting readings from electricity and other normal sources of EMF. In fact, I actually used a TriField Meter to find faulty wiring. You can walk around with this meter, which is an advantage.

TriField Natural

While the TriField meter was designed to pick up magnetic fields put out by technology, the TriField Natural EM meter is set to sense fields put out by natural, non-technological sources. But there is another major difference between the two meters. The TriField Natural meter can not be walked around with—contrary to what you may have seen folks doing on television. In magnetic mode, the Trifield Natural measures changes in the natural fields, which means that simply moving the meter around will cause it to detect change. The Trifield Natural can pick up living people—although not everyone and not all the time. People put out varying strengths of magnetic fields, which varies from day to day. Because moving a TriField Natural Meter around picks up the field changes caused by moving the device through the fields, they are only useful after setting them down and waiting a few seconds.

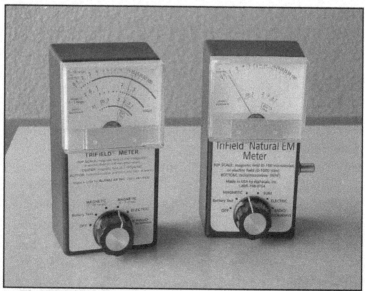

The TriField (left) and the TriField Natural EM Meter (right).

GEOMAGNETOMETER

THERE IS AN APPARENT CONNECTION between the Earth's magnetic field and psychic experiences, so measuring the local geomagnetic field can be extremely useful. A hand held geomagnetometer can pick up the Earth's magnetic fields. Interestingly, it looks as if not all the fields sensed by this device come from the Earth. For example, sometimes an upstairs bedroom will register a strong field, while the room below, closer to the ground, does not. Geomagnetometers are pricier than the TriField series, so not many folks use them.

TEMPERATURE SENSORS

PEOPLE OFTEN REPORT experiencing cold spots when having encountered ghosts. Measuring temperature changes can help us determine whether the cold spots are physical or only within our subjective perceptions. Most often, cold spots seem to be a construct of our experiences of apparitions or hauntings—like a cold chill we might feel when scared by a horror film.

In some situations, the temperature does physically change and can be measured. Naturally, the investigation must include a check for non-paranormal explanations for a drop in temperature. Often, no explanation can be found,

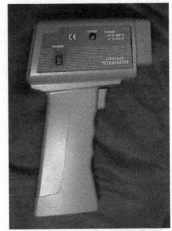

Non-contact Infrared Thermometers detect variations in surface temperature.

especially when the drop in temperature is connected to a witness's perception of a ghost.

There are a variety of thermometers we can use, but most ghost hunters use digital thermometers, of which there are many available. The better thermometers measure only the immediate area to determine where a cold spot starts and ends. This means the sensor must be moved around the room.

INFRARED

NON-CONTACT INFRARED THERMOMETERS, that measure temperature at a distance, have also been used by paranormal investigators. One advantage of this device is that it does not have to be physically moved from spot to spot. Non-contact thermometers send out a beam of infrared energy, which can only gives the temperature of the surfaces the beam hits. It does not measure the actual temperature of the air that the beam travels through.

THERMALVISION

ON OCCASION, I HAVE USED an infrared thermalvision camera in investigations. These special video cameras take thousands of temperature readings in an area. The display looks like something out of a scifi film. People's images show up on the monitor in various colors depending on their temperature and how much heat leaks through their clothing. According to the manufacturers instructions, these devices need some kind of surface from which to reflect the infrared sensors, though floating pockets of certain gases can also serve as surfaces.

I used thermalvision in a couple of cases in Florida, where we were looking for cold spots, which would have shown up as darker than the rest of the environment. We were surprised when we looked into the screen to see floating heat anomalies— pulsing areas hotter than the room. These "heat fogs" appeared at the same time that Aiko Gibo—a psychic from Japan who was assisting us—said the ghost of a little girl was present. The human reading was corroborated by heightened energy readings from several different frequency-weighted magnetometers, a microwave detector, and a Geiger counter. All pointed to the same source location—below Mrs. Gibo's right hand, which itself showed as hotter than the rest of her body. Mrs. Gibo's experience under-scored this. She said that the girl's ghost was tug-ging her right hand.

The reaction of Mrs. Gibo's hand could be explained as a change in blood flow to the hand. However, that such a variety of devices were detecting *something* at the same time and from the same spot as Mrs. Gibo's perceptions is most signifi-cant. Correlating several devices and a person's perceptions is the ideal. This is what ghost hunt-ers are looking for. A single device registering something out of the ordinary carries less credibility and is certainly less interesting than Mrs. Gibo's stated experience.

The author checking for magnetic anomalies.

LINK READINGS TO EXPERIENCE

READINGS FROM THE DEVICES, regardless of how high-tech or sci-fi must be correlated to a human experience of some kind of phenomena to even suggest we are picking up "ghosts." Without the connection to human experience, all we have are purely environmental anomalies—which themselves might be responsible for a person feeling "weird" or "strange." But it is no ghost and no haunting, just a feeling caused by energy in the system.

Technological tools are useful in an investigation only in so far as they are used in conjunction with the perceptions of the people present. Sometimes investigators include a sensitive or psychic who has demonstrated skill in sensing *something* at the same time as the devices or the witnesses. The sensitive is utilized much like a low-tech tool. The advantage is that we can ask questions for further clarification. Our human sensors provide deeper insight in to the cause of the phenomena by considering their own perceptions in a haunting case and by attempting communication with an apparition, if one seems to be present.

16

CAMERAS

ARDLY A MONTH GOES BY **that someone doesn't send me a photo or two with something on it, asking that I say what that something is.** People present when the photo was taken, including the photographer, usually did not experience anything paranormal at the time. Nor were they in a location where any witnesses said the place was haunted.

After I rule out basic photographic errors I usually tell to the sender: "It was most likely caused by some reflection or other photo-related issue, given that there's no connection to any experience, past or present, of a ghost or haunting. But, there's no way to be sure."

As with environmental readings, an unusual photo or video—by itself—is not an indication of a ghost or haunting. There must be a connection to human perception to consider labeling a location as haunted or having an apparition.

Ghost Photos

LET'S EXAMINE THE POSSIBILITY of a ghost being photographed by a camera. An apparition is some form of consciousness that does not reflect light. If it did reflect light everyone present would see it and cameras would capture it on film or digitally. But if it doesn't reflect light, how can a ghost be photographed or videotaped? How can one camera record something, but not others? Perhaps ghosts can psychokinetically affect the film or videotape, in some cases, willing something to appear on recording media. Perhaps it is a form of PK similar to the cases where apparitions are able to mentally move objects.

If a photo or videotape of a ghost is recorded in a location where no one has seen or sensed a ghost at the time, there's nothing to connect the recorded anomaly with a ghost and we must automatically look to other possible explanations for the anomaly.

On the other hand, when a photo or videotape is recorded in a place that has had past ghost sightings, greater weight can be given to the possibility that the image relates to a ghost.

A fake spirit photo, easily created with reflection off an aluminum foil ball by investigator Dave Manganelli.

EXPECTATIONS

IF GHOSTS CAN AFFECT FILM AND TAPE through PK, can the camera operator also affect film and tape? We do, after all, have more evidence that living people can do PK, than for ghosts to have PK.

Parapsychological research has shown that living people can affect film, videotape, and computers. In most photo and video cases, there is no experience of a ghost or spirit being present at the time of the image being captured. Therefore, it may be more likely that a living mind is responsible for such anomaly—at least we know the living person is there.

Don't look to PK as the most likely explanation for photographed anomalies. It is true that in a cemetery, expectation is at its height and perhaps this expectation can trigger PK. But investigators should always look for the simplest natural explanation first. For example there is lots of dust on dry nights and there's moisture on wet or humid nights. Both dust and moisture can reflect a flash, which are known to create round shapes on film. This is prevalent with digital cameras.

Sources of reflection don't need to be in the range of the viewfinder of the camera, by the way. They need only be in range of the flash or other source of light. That is, the reflection merely needs to be at angles the lens will pick up

GHOSTLY SUBSTANCE

SOME GHOST HUNTERS HAVE SUGGESTED THAT GHOSTS actually do have substance, or at least energy, that can be photographed, but that the ghost may be moving or vibrating too fast for the normal eye to see, or for cameras to photograph except at a fast shutter speed or when they happen to be snapped at just the right moment.

There are inherent flaws in this argument. Unless there is a human experience of the something being an apparition to correlate with the captured image, they may be snapping pictures of some previously unknown physical/energy effect. If so, that is worthy of it's own study. Photographed orbs and vortices are just as likely to be some other undiscovered natural phenomena, if true anomalies and not photographic irregularities.

DIGITAL MANIPULATION

PHOTOGRAPHIC AND VIDEO MANIPULATION is always a possibility that is hard to rule out. Computer programs that allow for enhancement, morphing, and other manipulation of photographic and video images are readily available.

Footage and photos I have seen generally fall into a few categories. There are those photos and videotapes taken that show some anomalies that are the result of photographic problems such as lens flares, reflections, unnoticed lighted, reflective objects in the environment, and the like. Digital cameras seem prone to these reflection-created orbs and other shapes.

Digital cameras are also often equipped with an infrared function to help with focus and flash settings. Even with the flash off or blocked, should the infrared pulse it is reflected back at the camera. Many digital cameras translate this reflected infrared light into a blue or white colored image.

Another category includes those photos of unusual, though natural, phenomena such as earth lights and ball lightning. Earth lights appear to be forms of static electricity thought to be generated by particular minerals in the ground. Ball lightning is a bundle of electrical energy that science still doesn't quite understand. Both forms of energy display can vary in size, strength and temperature, move at varying speeds, though often rather slowly, and appear outdoors or indoors. They have been seen as orbs and even flattened balls or disc-shaped objects. They have been know to even vary in color.

I've also seen photographic images that are probably caused by PK by the expectations of the photographer or other person present so that something odd to appears. Maybe the photographic anomaly is just another way for the subconscious to blow off steam or de-stress as with other poltergeist effects.

There are those photographic recordings that relate to the same environmental anomaly that allow us living folks to pick up on the history of a location. Haunting phenomena, sometimes called place memory, are often linked to human perceptions. However, magnetometers can pick up unusual physical readings—why not a camera?

Each possible explanation must be analyzed carefully. Explanations other than "It's a spirit!" must be considered first when there are no corroborating experiences of an apparition or haunting. Without a human witness to define the phenomenon as a ghost there are too many other possibilities to simply say a piece of film or video shows the image of a ghost.

BRING CAMERAS

DO BRING ALONG CAMERAS. Use digital cameras, but also bring a 35mm and use both as much as possible. Take pictures of the location, which can be used later to help make sense of what the witnesses tell you, and can help as reference in figuring out what did and did not happen.

The better the camera and lens—this usually means more expensive—the less likely there will be reflection-caused defects in the photographs. It is a misconception that cheap cameras are better because they have fewer bell and whistles and are less subject to manipulation. This last generalization may be true. However, cheaper cameras are more likely to have lenses and processes that do not correct for other problems.

Be careful there are no point sources of light, such as bright spot lights or candle flames on the periphery of the camera's view. Slight movements of the camera when you snap the picture can cause light-streaks and patterns to appear.

Documenting Interviews

VIDEO CAMERAS ARE USEFUL TO DOCUMENT INTERVIEWS with witnesses, if they're willing. Otherwise audio tape interviews. It helps to get a video record of the location because you can get more on video tape than on a photograph from a still camera. Of course, video has the advantage of having an audio track as well. Shoot footage as you walk around the location and when asking witnesses or psychics or other investigators to provide commentary.

One last thing: *Always* take readings, including pictures and video, of the spots where the hauntings occur, or where apparitions have been seen. More importantly, when someone is seeing or sensing something in the present time, take a picture or two of that spot, as well as anywhere they point. Also, take pictures or video of spots that register higher than the rest of the location on other detection devices. Then look for correlations between witness experiences and the images and other readings from environmental sensors.

17

AUDIO RECORDERS

SING DIGITAL AND ANALOG AUDIO RECORDERS
to capture the apparent voices of spirits is
surging in popularity. This process is by no
means new—it's been around for decades.
The sounds and voices recorded are called
Electronic Voice Phenomena—or EVP.

There's evidence that apparitions and
hauntings may affect audiotape, digital audio, and
the audio track on videotape. Ghost hunters listen to
audio recordings made during an investigation to
note unusual, unidentified voices, or other noises.
This is a long, arduous process. Then the data found
is correlated with data from other detection devices—
especially human experience.

MULTIPLE RECORDERS

NOTE I SAID *UNIDENTIFIED* VOICES OR NOISES. It's extremely important to note everyone in the room as
well as everyone anywhere near the room in which
you are recording. If the microphone is sensitive, it
can pick up voices and sounds from out of earshot,
as well as voices and sounds you and the other
investigators did not notice. Having a second recording device running simultaneously will help. Generally if both recorders do record the same voices and

sounds, it's not likely to be anything paranormal, even when you didn't hear the sounds yourself.

Sometimes recorders pick up radio signals—although with current technology this is less frequent. I have heard many recordings from investigations that sounded like a TV or radio playing from far in the background—even from a house next door.

Most EVP recordings I have heard have been of mumbling and garbled voices. The people playing the recording have already decided the voice says, "Hello" or some other specific phrase, while to others it sounds unintelligible. The recording is something akin to an auditory inkblot test, with the listener consciously or unconsciously hearing what he or she would *like* it to say. Some of these folks can be heard asking questions out loud, with the ostensible EVP "answering" the question—or at least following the question, since it's not apparent what the answer actually is.

As with photos, audio recordings, in and of themselves, cannot be pointed to as an indication that a ghost is communicating. There is no way to identify the source of the voice-like sounds. On occasion, EVP voices can be connected to unconsciously produced low-volume responses, called subvocalizing, by the questioner or other living folks present.

Usefulness of EVP

In combination with other devices and experiences of human witnesses and sensitives, EVP can be an additional good tool in the investigator's arsenal. EVP captured in a location that has been shown to have current haunting or apparitional experiences has more evidentiary value than EVP captured in places like cemeteries, where night birds, bugs, breezes, and other natural sounds are generally prevalent in the background. EVP captured closer in time to actual experiences of the haunting content or the apparition is more desirable. Best are recordings made at the *same time* as an experience or the registration of anomalies by other sensors.

In the Florida case with Mrs. Gibo, that I mentioned previously, something quite unusual happened. At close to 11:45 P.M. on the first night, following the incident in which Mrs. Gibo sensed the girl tugging her hand at the same time that several devices recorded anomalies, and make Mrs. Gibo was still "talking" with the ghost, I heard what sounded like screams of a young girl from somewhere outside the house.

No one else heard the screams—and there were more than a dozen people present, including the witnesses, investigators, and two TV crews. I ran outside to see if I could find any sign of anyone or anything. Nothing. Coming back inside, I explained what I'd heard. Everyone—including Mrs. Gibo—verified that nothing was heard.

The TV crews played back the video footage. We had several live microphones, with three cameras recording. Screams could be heard on one and only one camera. Even more interesting, the geomagnetic sensing station we had set up in the house showed a significant deviation—enough to make us have to recalibrate the device—just moments before I heard the screams.

In other cases with apparitions, we have gotten what sounded like human voices—though generally unintelligible—on the audio track of the video—again at the same time as someone was experiencing some perception of an apparition or as our other gear was detecting something, or both.

Alcatraz, a site with an abundance of place-memory.

When not all recording devices or people pick up the voices or sounds, we're left with an awkward conclusion. For a ghost's voice to appear on tape without otherwise being heard or recorded by back-ups, the ghost would have affected the one recorder directly, essentially putting the voice on tape. By definition, this is a psychokinetic effect.

But while we consider that a ghost was engaged in PK, we also consider the possibility that the intentions of living persons in the environment were responsible. PK research has also indicated that people can in some way affect audio tape and other digital recording media. Expectations of investigators must be considered as a possible influence. This dilemma is why we *must* look for other corroborating factors, whether human perception of the apparition or other devices sensing some environmental anomaly. Of course, it's not a given fact that any recorded anomaly is a ghost.

HAUNTING EVP

BOTH HAUNTINGS AND APPARITIONS CAN AFFECT RECORDERS. In some haunting cases, audio recordings of some facet of the anomalous events have actually been recorded. A colleague of mine, author and investigator Jon Saint-Germain, shared a tape recording with me of multiple voices and screams associated with a haunting he investigated in Tennessee. The recording was made while Jon and a radio personality were in a basement where people have reported hearing screams and voices associated with a past event. At the time neither Jon nor other witnesses heard the voices. The second recorder they had running did not pick up the curious sounds.

I am aware of other haunting cases where similar recordings have been made. Apparently, *something* in the environment was picked up by the audio recorder—the same or similar *something* that repeats in patterns and that people might perceive.

EXPLANATIONS OF EVPs

THE FIRST STEP IS TO ELIMINATE other normal sources of noise and voices. After that there are several possibilities: PK by the apparition, PK by a living person who is present, or a place memory—haunting—interacting with the recording device.

There have been promises of creating devices that allow apparitions to actually converse with the living. So far, credibility falls apart on close examination. At their best, EVP recordings are an indication that something is happening—something that needs further study. It is this exciting possibility that cries out for research and the development of better technology.

18

PREPARING FOR AN INVESTIGATION

DVANCE PREPARATION FOR YOUR INVESTIGA-
TION **is important. It can mean the
difference between a smooth investiga-**
tion or a three-ring circus.

ASSEMBLE A TEAM

IT IS GOOD TO HAVE OTHERS TO HELP with
interviewing witnesses. Witnesses should be interviewed
as many times as seems necessary– alone and in a
group. As new data and ideas are gathered you'll need
to interview witnesses about these developments. Having
more than one investigator on the team allows for
interviews from different perspectives. Having a second,
third, and even fourth investigator makes interviewing
go more smoothly, with more data collected.

When you come to the point when you try to
assess what you've learned and come to a conclusion,
other investigators make the thought processes that go
into analyzing your findings and shaping conclusions
much more dynamic. You can bounce ideas off one
another to better explore possibilities, and to come to a
consensus.

It is also helpful to bring in other people for the
assessment discussion, even if they were not involved in
the on-site the investigation. Having many eyes to view
the environment helps you see more.

Safety is another consideration. You can not be sure of everything you've been told or how safe it is. People who sound perfectly sane and composed on the phone can be quite disturbed. I have found myself in a couple of domestically volatile situations in which the husbands—not poltergeists—were abusing their wives.

While ghosts can't hurt you, you can encounter real physical danger from the people involved with the cases that find their way to a ghost hunter. Don't go alone.

GET CONSENT

MAKE SURE ALL PARTIES ARE AWARE of and have given their consent for your visit and the possibility of an investigation. When an investigation is a surprise to witnesses or non-witness residents it can cause tension and in some instances can bring the investigation to a halt.

Obviously, having someone at the location give you or witnesses a hard time is to be avoided. It makes the investigation difficult if not impossible and can inhibit witnesses in reporting their experiences.

Think broadly about who may be impacted by your investigation. For example, if the property is rented by witnesses, it may be important to interview the owner who can give a historical background on the place. They may be leery of talking to investigators if they have not been informed about the situation from the start.

Always make sure to get permission of all residents to avoid any trespassing charge.

The Winchester Mystery House in San Jose, California is one of America's strangest houses and haunted by the former owner.

PUBLIC HAUNTINGS

JUST BECAUSE A PLACE IS "PUBLIC' DOESN'T MEAN you can march in with your investigative team. Before getting a group together to investigate a publicly accessible location, such as an historical site, a restaurant, or a public building, it's *essential* that you gain full permission to conduct the investigation at the site. Contact the building management or the owner, explain why you want to conduct an investigation and the procedure you will follow. Ask for help in accessing witnesses for interviews.

Do not simply go to the site and roam around with detections meters, clicking away with cameras. Doing so can generate bad feelings in the people working there, and deter the owner from cooperating with any future investigators.

Always first confirm that there is actually something currently happening at the site. Just because a place looks spooky or is abandoned doesn't make it haunted and full of ghosts. Apparition, haunting, and poltergeist cases tend to happen in places populated by living people. For a valid investigation you need witnesses, and an indication that odd things are still happening. Without this, all you have is a spooky place or a place that once seemed to be haunted.

AVOID PUBLICITY

AS MUCH AS POSSIBLE, AVOID PUBLICITY. An investigation can easily get out of hand and turn into a media circus. Publicity brings gawkers who can disturb the situation, causing an upheaval in the lives of the people involved. Begin your investigation in an unobtrusive and low-key manner to not disturb the dynamics and relationships that may be causing the events.

Sarah Winchester's bedroom in the Mystery House.

ESTABLISH GROUND RULES

ESTABLISH GROUND RULES FOR MEDIA PARTICIPATION. The folks involved must okay the press being there. Reporters must be unobtrusive and abide by an agreement that you are in charge of the investigation. TV crews, when respectful of the people involved, can be helpful in documenting what's happening—though they do tend to be intrusive.

When the press does participate, you will probably have to promise to let them in on your conclusions before sharing them elsewhere. Take time to educate media personnel as to how they may be disruptive of the investigation. Generally the media respond well to being informed.

If the media hasn't already been contacted, ask that the family not do so. Generally this is no problem, as most people would rather remain anonymous.

If the family does alert the press without telling you first, consider that their motives are probably different from simply seeking help. They may be hoping for a book or movie deal. Avoid these cases because such motives may indicate exaggerated reports and even trickery and it's unlikely you'll get anything out of any movie deals.

AVOID UNINVITED INVESTIGATORS

KEEP OUT OTHER WOULD-BE INVESTIGATORS unless you are familiar with their methods and feel comfortable about having them there. For example, local psychics, ghost hunters or clerics may try to horn in on your investigation and be disruptive. They may talk about orbs, demons, or exorcisms and contaminate witness reports. Often they are publicity seekers and they will make a circus of your investigation and a mess of the family's situation.

Sarah's handyman has been seen in the front gardens of the Winchester Mystery House.

AVOID DEBUNKERS

WATCH OUT FOR DEBUNKERS because they usually denounce the witnesses' experiences and get in the way of the investigation. They often make statements like, "They're only hallucinating" or "They're simply suggestible," which damages the psychology of the situation. While sometimes true, debunkers' statements upset witnesses and invalidate their experiences.

Another problem with debunkers is that they may bring in the media without permission of the family members. Typically, they are seeking to gain personal publicity, and generally have little empathy for what the family is going through.

19

WITNESSES

HENEVER POSSIBLE, interview witnesses at the location of the anomalous events. Doing so enables you to
observe their behavior as you interview them. If you can't interview
witnesses on site, interview them as
soon as possible after your the initial visit to the
site. Also interview non-witness residents or employees
of the place where the events have taken place.
Some of these folks can provide insight into what's
going on even though they did not have any direct
experience of the phenomena.

PROBE DEEPLY

THE BEST INVESTIGATORS ASK A MULTITUDE OF QUESTIONS
to get a full picture of what's going on. Sometimes
the dynamics at work are obvious. Many times,
however, the issues behind a ghost's appearance or
the stresses that trigger a poltergeist scenario are less
than obvious. The phenomena may be symbolic of
the underlying causes. It helps to be excessively
curious.

Be persistent with your questions. Repeatedly
question the specifics in various ways to see if the

experience's features remain the same or how it changes in repeated tellings. It may be that the same question worded differently will trigger different memories about the experience. Asking the same question in different ways also enables you to see how consistent the experience is for each person. Typically imagined and misperceived details tend to change a bit in the retelling.

Ask questions that will help you form a good picture of the actual goings-on. Remember not to jump to immediate conclusions that the events are paranormal. Always dig for normal explanations, such as deception, problems with the electrical system, or earth movements, before concluding that the cause is paranormal.

Questions about one type of phenomena are not necessarily applicable to other kinds. Some questions are more applicable to hauntings than poltergeist cases. A haunting, for example, generally has no physical components, so asking, "How often do things move around?" would be irrelevant in such a case.

Who, What, When, Where, and How

ASK QUESTIONS THAT IDENTIFY WHO WAS AROUND before, during, or right after the events. Ask who witnessed what and what was going on before and at the time of each specific occurrence of the event. Ask how people felt before, during, and after each event. Such questions help define the general patterning of the disturbances and experiences. You may need to repeat questions you asked during the initial phone call when you are on site to get a better handle on what's going on.

Ask witnesses *their* opinion of what's going on and who may be connected to it. Whether they know it or not, witnesses often have insight into the causes of phenomena. Be discerning, however, and consider witnesses' opinions in light of what you know about apparitions, hauntings, and poltergeists. Witnesses beliefs and fears can get in the way.

As you listen to witnesses respond to your questions, make sure to consider the physical location and possible factors in the environment that may have promoted the events.

INTERACTIONS AND SYMBOLS

REPORTED INCIDENTS MAY BE SYMBOLIC of underlying psychological and interpersonal dynamics, especially in poltergeist cases. Think of the disturbances as dreams come to life and look for the symbolic meaning of the experiences in much the same way that you would consider a dream element to be a metaphor for a real issue. For example an ashtray may have flown across the room. Ask witnesses for their opinions as to why that item was "chosen," how and where it flew, and if it broke. Asking witnesses—especially the individual who may be the agent—such questions can lead to revealing answers.

In one poltergeist case I investigated, bursts of water were related to the agent's emotional struggles around his parents pushing him to be on the school's swim team. He didn't want to be on the team, which his parents refused to accept. In another case, water symbolized suppressed grief. Small flames have popped up in a colleague's case, which represented the agent's pent-up anger.

It may be helpful explore the lives of the people involved—their relationships and history as a family or work group—to get an overall picture of how to deal with the phenomena.

Ask what the specific events and the case as a whole might represent. Suggest to witnesses that they look at the situation as a dream, and then discuss the case from that perspective. Ask what stresses they may have felt before, during and after the events. Also ask how the occurrences of the phenomena has affected them.

20

DATA

HE ULTIMATE GOAL IS OF THE INVESTIGATION **determines whether gathering data or helping resolve the situation takes precedence.** Generally a family reports phenomena because they want it to stop. Professional ghost hunters, on the other hand, want to learn something about psychic phenomena and hope to personally experience the anomaly. The client's needs should always take priority over those of the investigator. This may mean sacrificing your potential experiences to help the distraught family. Data-gathering is important in any case, even when the situation calls for a quick resolution. After the anomalous events have ceased, it is usually possible to learn about what went on and why it happened by studying the data collected.

PERCEPTIONS IMPORTANT

TAKE NOTE OF ANY UNUSUAL PERCEPTIONS reported by anyone—both witnesses and members of your team—during the investigation. These are added to the other information gathered from witnesses to assess what's going on and what to do about it. Take notes on perceptions of psychics you may have brought with you, for example. Because these are sensed as you are investigating, there is immediacy about psychics perceptions that you may not gain from the witnesses. Pay attention to your own perceptions as well and take notes on anything unusual that you may experience.

DATA FROM DEVICES

DATA GATHERED FROM TECHNOLOGICAL DEVICES must be considered in the context of data gathered from human experience. This includes the experiences of the witnesses at the time of the anomalous events, along with perceptions of investigators, psychics, and witnesses experienced at the time the recordings were made by the devices.

Consider all possible explanations of the events, including potential perceptual misinterpretations, belief biases, and coincidence. Consider rare and unusual but normal explanations, such as infrasound.

LOOK FOR PATTERNS

LOOK FOR RELATIONSHIPS AMONG THE EXPERIENCES reported, the recordings from tech devices, and the people involved. Notice patterns in the physical data, along with psychological factors. Identifying patterns and relationships helps in many ways. They help you decide if you're dealing with an apparition, a poltergeist, or a haunting— or some combination.

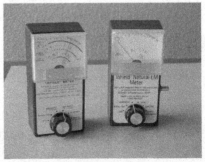

Magnetic field detection meters.

Patterns point to who seems most connected to the phenomena. By following that person's actions closely, you have a better chance of observing or experiencing something anomalous. Patterns help pinpoint when and where events are likely to happen—so you can be there "next time." Patterns connect normal experiences to paranormal interpretations so as to allow for a better normal versus paranormal assessment.

Blend in

BECOME PART OF THE SETTING AS MUCH AS POSSIBLE and blend into the background, especially in lengthy investigations. Your presence changes the ambiance and may disrupt factors allowing the phenomena to happen. It is important to minimize this unavoidable effect. Similarly, any equipment used for continuous monitoring should be as unobtrusive as possible.

Use Field Experiments

EMPLOY FIELD EXPERIMENTS WHEN APPROPRIATE. A field experiment is a reconstruction of reported events utilizing patterns around the phenomena that have been identified.

For example, you might put everyone in the same places they were when they saw the apparition and reenact the motions of the experience as they reported it. Strive to recreate the same conditions as when an apparition was seen or when an object moved. In a haunting or apparition case, see if all witnesses get the same perceptions of the presence by having them describe what is seen and heard during the reenactment. Also have witnesses select adjectives from a checklist like the one in this chapter that help describe the witnesses' perceptions of the personality of the presence.

Field experiments involving reconstruction may be inappropriate—especially in poltergeist cases—because they can increase the stress witnesses experience and exacerbate psychological and emotional issues. Using the Anomalous Experience Checklist is generally experienced as "safe" by witnesses and in many cases helps to soothe the anxiety by being able to identify it on paper.

CHARACTERISTICS OF PHENOMENA

PARAPSYCHOLOGIST DR. GERTRUDE SCHMEIDLER PIONEERED the checklist method for field research that many investigators find quite useful. By providing witnesses with lists of words to be associated with the apparition or haunting, investigators can look for correlations between the experiences of the witnesses. Such correlations are found in most haunting and apparition cases. The results from the use of such lists can provide a good picture of an apparition's personality—even emotional motivations.

The Anomalous Experience Checklist was adapted and expanded from one used by Dr. Schmeidler and Dr. Thelma Moss. Add any descriptive adjectives that you find relate to the activities that the presence, or ghost seems to be carrying out, or are associated with its personality, behavior, or emotions. Ask witnesses and others with whom you use the checklist to do the same.

An approach that I have found useful is to have two groups walk through and then complete the Checklist exercise. Witnesses, along with anyone else who knows about the case comprise one group. The other group is made up of people having no knowledge of the specifics of the situation. Another possibility is to do the exercise with groups of psychics versus skeptics or groups of believers versus disbelievers. By comparing the results between groups, you can determine to what degree, if any, the groups detect the phenomena without the impact of suggestion playing a big role.

Keep others completing the Checklist away from the witnesses, whether they experienced something or not. You must avoid people comparing their responses to the Checklist until after you have compiled a composite of the checklist responses.

ANALYZING CHECKLIST DATA

NOTE WHICH ADJECTIVES WERE CIRCLED or crossed out by the majority in the group. This gives a reflection of the degree to which people experienced the same things in the same place, and the consensus as to what the perceived events or apparitions look like as well as what factors may be related.

The composite checklist will enable you to create a picture of what may be going on. It points to where to dig for more information. It may be helpful for you to complete the Checklist yourself—whether you've experienced something or not. You and your fellow ghost hunters may be picking up information with your psi abilities. Another possibility is to have one or more professional psychics complete the checklist exercise. This will reveal if they are picking up the same things as the witnesses. Secondarily, it helps gauge how useful they are to your investigation.

ANOMALOUS EXPERIENCE CHECKLIST

Instructions: Circle those items on the list that seem to relate to the ghost's activity or intent as you experienced it. Cross out those terms that are opposite to how you experienced the ghost or presence. Ignore terms that are not applicable to your experience. Write comments or explanations next to the terms that relate to your experience or on the reverse of the sheet. Also write a brief description of feelings, emotions, physical sensations, or sights, sounds, smells or other sensations that you get when the presence is around or when "things happen."

Afraid
Angry
Annoying someone
Attacking someone
Attention getting
Bored
Building something
Cautious
Cold
Compassionate
Cooking something
Communicating
Crazy
Crying
Curious
Dancing
Depressed
Eating
Fearful
Floating above the ground
Flying in the air
Fun-Loving
Gesturing
Getting rid of someone/thing

Happy
Harassing someone
Helping someone
Hiding
Humorous
Insulting someone
Intelligent
Laughing
Lonely
Looking around
Loving
Lying down
Mischievous
Mocking
Moving in a direction
Musing
Needy
Needs help
Non-feeling
Non-thinking
Obnoxious
Pacing restlessly
Passive
Peering

Playful

Playing a musical instrument

Playing a game

Protective of someone

Protective of something

Purposeful

Pursuing someone

Puttering around

Reading

Repairing something

Resting

Restless

Running

Sad

Sarcastic

Searching for someone/thing

Sensual

Serious

Sewing

Shy

Singing

Sitting

Standing up

Stealing something

Stern

Talkative

Talking

Threatening someone

Trapped

Vengeful

Violent

Walking

Wandering aimlessly

Wanting

Wants help

Warm

Writing

INTRODUCE CONTROLS

INTRODUCE CONTROLS TO BE SURE people are not rigging things or deliberately causing objects to move. Be subtle when introducing controls. Do it gradually and inconspicuously because such actions can suggest disbelief on your part, which may prevent phenomena from occurring in your presence or upset the psychodynamics of the situation. Check and update the controls frequently to make sure they're not subverted.

KEEP NOTES

IT'S IMPORTANT TO KEEP DETAILED NOTES along with all recording from devices. Review your notes from time to time during and after the investigation. Write down impressions you or the other investigators have as you investigate. Make note taking easy. For example, you might provide each investigator with a tape recorder and a good supply of tapes. Bring a camera to photograph the pertinent parts of the location as well as the whole place. This provides a frame of reference when going over the specifics of the case.

Bring plenty of pads for taking notes and for sketching. Always include a measuring tape in your ghost hunting gear. It helps to draw a floor plan of the environment and to plot where the phenomena occurred and where everyone was located at the time. These extra bits will prove invaluable in your final assessment.

CHECK FACTS

CHECK AND RECHECK ALL FACTS OF THE CASE. It may make sense to do a bit of digging into outside sources of information. You might, for example, look into the background history of the location and the persons appearing as an apparition.

Doing background checks of the people involved may make sense especially if there is a question in your mind that something may be missing or when facts conflict. For example, if a witness says he is under the care of a doctor, get permission to check with the doctor to find out the facts of the aliment.

When it seems pertinent information on the family history, including history of mental illness. You'll need to be tactful in this exploration.

CONSULT EXPERTS

CONSULTING EXPERTS IN OTHER FIELDS MAY BE NEEDED. For example, a magician might give you suggestions on how to set up controls against deception in a poltergeist case. A builder may explain why odd sounds are produced by the house. A geologist can explain effects that could be related to unstable foundation of the house or to odd temperature readings, which might be caused by an underground water supply.

SEVERAL VISITS

YOUR INVESTIGATION MAY REQUIRE SEVERAL VISITS, or even warrant staying on-location for an extended period of time. Additional visits increase the possibility of being present when the anomalous events occur. You may need to return to the site to correlate events to the environment to get a better sense of what may be going on. This is especially true in poltergeist cases. Multiple visits may also be called for in long-term haunting and apparition cases in publicly accessible places, such as haunted restaurants.

21

DIAGNOSTICS

ATEGORIZING CASES IS NOT ALWAYS EASY **because they don't necessarily lend themselves to being put into neat little boxes.** Sometimes, the phenomena overlap and relate to more than one model of paranormal activity. Sometimes there may be a combination of unrelated phenomena occurring in the same place. Other times one phenomenon causes the occurrence of another one.

HAUNTINGS AND APPARITIONS

HAUNTINGS ARE RELATED TO THE ENVIRONMENT and imprints of human activity—so hauntings can occur just about anywhere. Of course, older locations offer more to choose from for the place memory.

Apparitions commonly appear in houses and other buildings that also may have residual imprints of past inhabitants. Sometimes, an apparition's appearance alters the environment enough to let loose an imprint so that the recording is "boosted," making it more evident. Perhaps whatever the apparition triggers in the witnesses that causes them to perceive a ghost allows them to perceive haunting impressions as well. This means investigators must assess each sighting of an apparition for evidence of apparent consciousness. For example, note if the figure walking down the hall is also interactive. Are the footsteps witnesses reported hearing caused by the apparition, or are some of the sounds haunting-related?

HAUNTINGS AND POLTERGEISTS

POLTERGEIST CASES CAN ALSO OCCUR IN HAUNTED PLACES. In some cases I've investigated, hauntings caused the stress that triggered the RSPK. People living in a haunted home may experience the haunt with or without the stress that generates a poltergeist. In other cases a haunting might be a secondary phenomenon happening in a place where a polter-geist agent became active, with the PK activity due to stress unrelated to the haunting factors. Most people seem to be not susceptible to becoming poltergeist agents, so in most cases the stress that comes from experiencing a haunting is not likely to cause a resident to become RSPK-active.

My colleagues and I have investigated a number of cases where it appeared that the haunting interacted with people in that environment and connected with witnesses in ways that did generate PK activity. Most often, however, the physical events that follow are directly related to the story present in the imprinted haunt. It's as though the unconscious mind of a living person taps into the history, which helps the reenactment along by causing things to move. Sometimes, someone—who might become a poltergeist agent in other stressful circumstances—reacts to the stress caused by the haunting and RSPK follows.

Poltergeists and Apparitions

There are poltergeist cases in which the agent unconsciously projects a mental image of a shadowy figure or other entity. This serves to deflect all blame for the activity away from the agent and onto a now-seen paranormal being. The projection is received telepathically by others in the situation.

Possibly an apparition is in the same location or hanging around with the people connected to a poltergeist case. The apparition may not have a causal relation to the poltergeist phenomenon. Then again, the encounters with the apparition may be stress points for the agent.

The careful ghost hunter looks at the overall case as well as at the individual incidents and people involved. All reported events are examined for all normal causes, unusual but non-paranormal causes, and for possible paranormal causes. Mixed-bag cases are quite common. You must figure out how much of the anomalous events can be explained by each of the possibilities, which of them need resolution, and how to integrate your explanations of the phenomena and experiences.

Coming to Conclusions

Investigating spontaneous cases of psi requires that a ghost hunter be a detective, a psychologist, a magician, an anthropologist, and a counselor. You must avoid jumping to conclusions until all the facts are in. You must understand the delicate psychological balances within individuals and between people, and how psychology of individuals and groups can manifest as psychic experience. You must eliminate normal or natural explanations for the experiences and perceptions. You must observe the beliefs of the people involved regarding psi. Where appropriate and when ethics demand it, you must help the people involved come to a resolution of the experience so that they integrate it into their lives in a positive fashion.

In mixed-bag cases involving multiple phenomena each phenomenon probably requires a separate solution. One phenomenon may need to be dealt with, while others do not. Be careful to never guarantee the removal or stoppage of paranormal phenomena or experiences. Don't over promise with a comment like, "We can take care of it for you." Instead, tell clients that the techniques you employ have been successful in the vast majority of cases—but there is no guarantee it will succeed in their case.

EXPLORE SYMBOLISM AND METAPHOR

DIG INTO THE MEANING THE INCIDENTS HOLD for the people involved. Anomalous events often symbolize issues in peoples' lives. Consider if an apparition represents someone real or if it was conjured up by the unconscious of one or more people involved in the case. Look for the patterns of the phenomena's occurrence. Look at the anomalous experiences as you would look at a dream—even though these experiences may be very real—to uncover the symbols and their possible meanings.

UNCOVER NEEDS

PERHAPS THE PHENOMENA POINT TO A WITNESS'S NEED to communicate about a deep issue or perhaps it serves to gain attention. Explore what the phenomena might be trying to say about someone's need. Consider if the phenomena are unrelated to the people experiencing it, as in many haunting cases where the events are related to the location and seem to be unrelated to the people. The fact that people are perceiving these past events indicates that there is something going on with the witnesses that causes them to perceive the information in the first place.

If witnesses are fearful of the phenomena it doesn't necessarily indicates a general fear of the paranormal. People may react fearfully in an unusual situation, yet when asked, express no real concern about ghosts. It may be a fear of being in danger or perhaps a fear of the unknown. Or it may be fear of something else that is expressed in the form of a paranormal experience.

Identify the verifiable information in the witness reports and match this with what you know about apparitions, hauntings and poltergeists. The objective is to determine if the information is verifiable by outside sources only, or if it was already in the minds of the witnesses before the anomalous events occurred. In the latter case, it's possible that the phenomena were enhanced by this prior knowledge.

Case analysis includes determining if the experiences of apparitions and hauntings truly reflect people and events from the past. Make sure to check facts and history carefully. Identify all channels of information to the people other than paranormal ones.

22

RESOLUTIONS

PLANS FOR RESOLUTION OF A CASE MUST BE TAILORED **to what is going on with the apparent phenomena, to the psychological** dynamics of the situation, and to the interpersonal relationships and social interactions involved.

If your goal was to provide conclusions to those involved and the curious, then your work may be done. If the site of the anomalous activity is a public place, you may want to work out a way to be kept notified of any new anomalous events that may occur in the place and arrange for return visits.

If the site is a private residence or workplace where the folks wanted an investigation because *they* were curious, fill them in on your findings and ask that they note any new experiences and keep you posted.

The vast majority of my cases have been situations in which the people had an adverse reaction to the ghost and wanted some kind of resolution. Usually, they wanted the ghost "busted" and made to leave. How you handle the people and help them with their experiences and their reactions requires further planning.

Ghost of a chaplain pops up in the chapel area of the USS Hornet.

GET THE BIG PICTURE

LOOKING AT ALL THINGS THAT POUR INTO THE WHOLE of any one case is vitally important. Studying the inter-personal relationships involved is as important as tracking where objects moved. Separating psychological effects from parapsychological ones is as important as separating out normal physical explanations from paranormal ones. Getting a whole picture means looking at the psyches of the people as you investigate events.

Having basic knowledge of psychology is essential. Psi experiences—whether cases of precognition or of RSPK—are bound up in the psychological dynamics of the persons involved. To learn why something is happening to people at this particular point in their lives may be the most important clue to how to integrate the experience into their lives or to stopping the phenomena from happening again.

PROVIDE USEFUL INFORMATION

THE PRESENCE OF AN INVESTIGATOR can sometimes change the dynamics of the situation enough to bring the phenomena to a halt, sometimes permanently. Even with the phenomena stopped, the experience will have had an impact on the people. They probably need to understand what went on and why it happened to feel at ease about the situation. Arming people with parapsychological information about psychic phenomena, including correcting misconceptions and fears the people may have regarding the phenomena is helpful. Even when the phenomena and experiences have not stopped, providing people involved with solid information about the paranormal can itself "bust" the ghost or a poltergeist. The simple act of helping people understand the underlying psychological dynamics of the happenings may cause the phenomena to come to a halt. Educating the witnesses about the phenomena can remove the fear and other adverse reactions and often bring an end to the anomalous events.

COUNSELING

COUNSELING IS PROBABLY CALLED FOR IN ANY CASE in which people have had a strong psychological reaction to what happened. On-site counseling is usually listening to people's concerns and educating them as to the possibilities—paranormal or otherwise. Listen attentively to the people reporting the experience and reassure them that many others have had such experiences. Particularly important is to let them know that having had such an experience doesn't indicate that they are "going crazy." Simply labeling the experience helps. For example, describing an experience as being clairvoyant can be quite calming—especially when followed with a summary of current views parapsychology about such experiences.

BRING A THERAPIST

BE CAREFUL ABOUT ADVICE-GIVING that could overstep
ethical and legal boundaries into territory covered by
trained counselors, therapists, and psychologists.
Should the initial information I gather indicate that
the case warrants it, I'll bring a licensed psychotherapist with me. On an investigation when it looks like
people have suffered psychological disturbance because
of their experiences, I refer them to counselors by
saying something like, "Counseling can help you deal
with your *reactions* to the phenomena."

People often express concern that maybe they are
going crazy and want to be certain this is not the
case and they generally want to make sure others
don't think they're crazy. It is important to recognize
that these experiences may not be psychic at all but
that psychological and/or neurological illness may be
responsible for hearing voices, feeling attacked, thinking one is possessed—even seeing ghosts.

I often refer people to their physicians to be
examined for possible neurological or other physiological illnesses. It can be difficult to explain to a
frightened person that "the voices you're hearing
might be related to something physiological." Make
sure to explain that "we need to eliminate all other
possibilities, including physiological ones, in order to
help you."

Make sure that the therapists are not scoffers of
the paranormal or otherwise negating the person's
experience because they have conflicting views of
paranormal experiences. It's important that the therapist is not afraid of ghosts or demons, and not
imposing personal religious beliefs on to the case.
On the other hand, sometimes I do refer people to

The office in the USS Hornet's Medical Bay, where the author has gotten cooperation from several ghosts.

religious counselors or involve them from the start if the religious beliefs of the witnesses seem to be blocking them from considering our explanations and advice.

The same advice goes for working with psychics. Many psychics have beliefs that would not be helpful if imposed on the individuals in a case, especially when they contradict what you've told the clients. On the other hand, many psychics have great counseling skills—though they should never portray themselves as counselors or therapists unless they are licensed.

23

EXPLORATIONS

GHOST HUNTERS MUST GRAPPLE with an ethical dilemma. Is it more important to the investigators to encourage the anomalous phenomena to continue to study its dynamics or is helping the people involved more important, which may mean doing whatever you can to stop the events from reoccurring? This can be a difficult choice for the investigator hoping to personally experience the paranormal occurrences. However, the ethics of the situation *demand* that the needs of the people involved come first. One takes a global view of the situation to see what the needs are and just what has to be accomplished to satisfy the family. If there are appropriate places where you can sink your teeth and bring out the phenomena without upsetting the psychological dynamics, pin those down and compare such issues against possible damage to the situation.

EXPLORE EMOTIONS

LOOK AT THE NEEDS OF THE FAMILY IN THEIR ENTIRETY, not just the needs of the individuals. You may have to get into delicate territory, including issues of repressed sexuality and other sexual tensions, which may be the causal link driving RSPK—especially when the phenomena is centered on or around the bed. You may be squeamish about probing into issues related to sex. However, to gather the information you need to help, you will sometimes have to probe such delicate topics to understand what the events symbolize. The RSPK allows the agents an alternate mouth for expressing things. It is a symbolic way to say something is wrong without coming out and confronting others directly. If you help get the issues out into the open the PK occurrences often stop.

Demonic Attacks

When people talk about demonic attacks, look for what or who the demon represents to the victim. Dream work provides techniques for interpreting nightmare elements in a dream. It can be helpful for you to study dream work processes. I'm not talking about merely using a "dream dictionary," although the symbolism they offer might be a starting point for further exploration in a specific case.

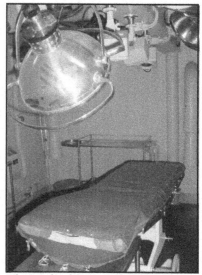

Sometimes people have a personal investment in believing the attacks come from some evil entity as a form of self-punishment or guilt. People who believe

The Medical Bay on the USS Hornet is the site of much emotion and many ghost encounters.

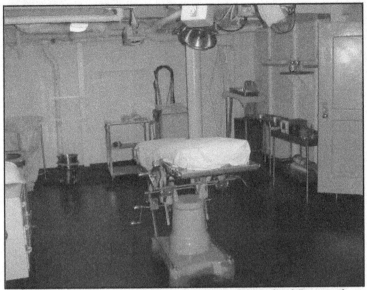

People perceive some negative emotion in the Medical Bay on the
USS Hornet—emotion imprinted from past events.

that they are being attacked by something outside themselves can be resistant to exploring other possibilities, especially when the most likely explanation that the demon has been conjured up by their own subconscious.

In the classic science-fiction film *Forbidden Planet*, the scientist's mind had been enhanced by ancient alien technology and manifests a monster from the ID to prevent him from being removed from the planet. The starship that comes to check on him is violently attacked. The monster gains more power each time the captain suggests they get off-world. Eventually the monster takes on a life of its own and attacks the scientist who created it. Thankfully, Earthbound poltergeist agents have not the power to press the phenomena to such an extreme degree!

It's exceedingly rare for a person to be attacked by an outside entity. Usually attacks are psychological, not physical. For this reason reports of physical attacks must be examined from the perspective of understanding what the attacks—and the demon— represent to the person attacked, and why they might think the attacks happened.

Hard questions must be asked and the answers examined. Unless the answers are obvious, a full-scope investigation of the overall case and the individual incidents is needed. The answers are often obvious—just be prepared for situations when they're not.

FEAR AND SENSITIVITY

BECAUSE OUR CULTURE DOES NOT ACCEPT APPARITION, poltergeist, or haunting scenarios as normal, people often react with fear. After anomalous events, some people become a bit more suggestible. A single sighting of an apparition, especially when frightening, can cause witnesses to conclude that just about everything unusual they experience is also caused by the ghost. They may become sensitive to sounds and sights in their home they'd not noticed before the anomalous events occurred. Such sounds include the noises the house makes at night as the temperature changes and the building settles. People may assign significance to coincidental events, or to normal physiological changes such as having a headache or becoming ill.

INVOLVE WITNESSES

INVOLVING THE WITNESSES IN THE INVESTIGATIVE PROCESS helps decrease their emotional distress because it soothes fear and stress. Often having these experiences causes witnesses to experience a sense of loss of control, which freaks them out. Tell witnesses to look for normal causes for the incidents. Instruct them to make a time line of the events and to keep a journal of anything new that happens. In an apparition or haunting case involve witnesses in researching the house and prior owners in the public records and local newspaper archives. Having an actual role in the investigation tends to remove the emotionality of their connection to the events and provides a sense of personal control.

Over the years, I've received a few report of someone seeing a ghost, only to realize that the ghost was oneself. Apparently their own actions left an imprint in the house that they subsequently saw. Just seeing a ghost can be disturbing. Realizing that you are the ghost can be quite overwhelming!

Consider all sides of the story, all data, and all possibilities. "I don't see any general prescription," said Karlis Osis, one of the leading field researchers of the late 20th Century. "Like people in therapy, it can be extremely different in different cases, depending on the background and depending also on the psychological makeup." Hearing this is not much comfort to someone who has just seen himself as a ghost. The experiences "are helped with cognitive enlightenment, " said Osis. "But I have not found that any particular formula would do. You have to see them where they are."

Depending on the case, resolution can be anywhere from quick and easy to long and drawn out. Much depends on the degree of acceptance by witnesses of your explanations and instructions. With an apparition, how well a technique works may depend on how stubborn the ghost is.

The USS Hornet Aircraft Carrier Museum.

There are times when nothing you do will resolve the situation. Fortunately, such stubborn cases are in the minority. It's usually the witnesses themselves who prevent resolutions. I've had cases in which the people were so attached to their belief system about the ghost that they could not accept a normal explanation—or that poltergeist phenomena could be caused by one of them. Sometimes people seemed to believe that ending the phenomena ended the feelings of being special and put them back in their mundane lives.

24

BUSTING POLTERGEISTS

N SOME WAYS, poltergeist cases are the easiest handle because they involve living people. The PK activity can be seen as a stress-relief valve. On the other hand, the psychology of the situation can be a delicate and complicated matter. After you have identified the agent and worked out ways to stop the RSPK activity, it's important the that poltergeist agent and others in the family deal with the stresses that set off the poltergeist.

The ghost hunter must assume the role of detective to figure out who is most likely to be the agent. The person always around when the phenomena happens is most likely to be the agent. Sometimes a particular combination of family members or coworkers triggers the stress on the agent that leads to the psychokinetic activity.

Follow The Stress

DETERMINING WHO IS LIKELY TO BE THE AGENT begins by determining who is under stress. Teenagers are the stereotypical agents because they are experiencing physiological and emotional stresses of puberty and adolescence. However, many of my cases involved people over 20, even some in their 70s. So just because a teenager is present, don't jump to the conclusion that the teen is the agent. Dig deeper to discover who is experiencing the related stress. Explore what the objects moving may represent to whom and who seeming to be always at the center of the events.

The RSPK creates a scenario in which a ghost, or poltergeist causes chaos. The poltergeist acts as a stress relief valve for the individual, while putting the blame and responsibility onto the unseen entity. In short, the subconscious mind of the agent gets to do what we would love to do when stressed out: throw and break things. Since it's socially unacceptable for the agent to throw and break things and doing so has unpleasant consequences, the agent's subconscious allows the stress to dispel by using PK to lash out.

What happens is usually the key to *who* is doing it as well as *why* they are doing it. If the kitchen appliances act up, perhaps there's resentment surrounding cooking or kitchen duties, for example. If a computer continually crashes when the agent is under a pressing deadline or if one has been forbidden to surf the Internet, the key is the stress issues around the use of the computer. Often poltergeist activities are very symbolic, like a flame equating to angry feelings. Sometimes the connections are obvious, as with a husband's treasured items being tossed and broken because of the wife's stress from the relationship with him.

Accepting Responsibility

Resolving the case can be as simple as getting agents to recognize that they are unconsciously causing the phenomena and to deal with those stresses. Accepting responsibility for the RSPK is the easiest way to get the agent's subconscious mind to stop its PK actions. It's a little like a child being caught acting up behind a parent's back.

Agent-acceptance can be difficult until the people in the case can accept 1) that such things are possible coming from a *living* mind; 2) that the living mind is one of one of the family members; 3) that one or more people—mainly the agent—is under stress that can cause PK activity; and 4) that the RSPK is probably coming from the person undergoing the most stress. I find it interesting that people can accept that a ghost or demon can toss furniture around, but resist the idea that the disturbances may be caused by PK from living people.

Resolution comes when the agent deals with the stress being experienced, and addresses the causes of that stress. This may mean individual counseling, and possibly counseling for the entire group. Sometimes dealing with the stress halts the RSPK even when the agent does not accept personal responsibility. I suggest that you identify the stress issues as soon as possible, and suggest counseling to alleviate that stress—perhaps even before trying to get the agent to accept responsibility for the PK. Dealing with the stress is a long-term solution. On occasion the agent's PK can act up with new stresses even when responsibility for the poltergeist has been accepted.

REENACT THE PK EXPERIENCE

INVESTIGATIONS HAVE HAD SUCCESS in having the agent—sometimes the entire family—consciously trying to move objects. While it's rare that anything psychokinetic will happen, the exercise seems to rechannel the energy from the stress.

You might have the agent and the others mentally focus on directing any object they see in motion and attempt to change its direction. Attempts at conscious PK seems to disperse the activity. Possibly doing so implies that one's mind may be involved in causing the phenomena, because by trying to do PK consciously people are confronted with the possibility that they might be responsible for the unconsciously-created PK.

PK EXERCISE

I'VE HAD SUCCESS WITH HAVING THE AGENT and family members do conscious PK exercises, such as a technique used successfully by the late science and science-fiction writer Martin Caidin.

Take a 3- or 4-inch square of paper, fold and crease it from corner to corner in both directions, so it forms a pyramid. Next, balance the pyramid on a spindle using a long needle or pin stuck up through a small block of wax or clay. When the pyramid target is balanced on the pin, lightly blow on it to make sure it spins.

Sit back and watch the pyramid for a minute or two to make sure your breathing and any air currents in the room don't cause it to turn. The pyramid should be quite still. Place your hands on either side of the pyramid, with palms facing it. Wait again to see if the warmth from your hands turns the pyramid. Again, it shouldn't turn.

Next, focus your attention on the pyramid and visualize it turning in either direction. See it moving in your mind. Don't concentrate, rather focus your attention on visualizing the pyramid turning. Caidin suggested tensing your muscles and bearing down on your hands while imagining the pyramid turning in your mind and thinking "Turn!"

Continue doing this for about 30 seconds to a minute. As you relax your arms and other muscles, relax your mind so you're not concentrating. The point is not to concentrate too hard but instead to keep the visualization of the turning pyramid going. With a number of tries most people are able to turn the pyramid.

Caidin had success with this technique and taught many others to do it. In fact, his students could put the pyramid under glass, which cut off all outside air currents, and they were still able to make it turn with mental visualization. I have had success teaching people to do this exercise.

When I've used the Caidin exercise in poltergeist cases, the RSPK stops fairly quickly. Only sometimes is the agent able to continue to do conscious PK. Nonetheless, the stress points causing the PK must be deal with for a complete resolution of the case.

25

EVICTING APPARITIONS

NTERACTION IS THE KEY FACTOR **in resolving apparition cases. The focus is on communicating with the ghost. The reason for** the ghost appearing can be learned by asking the ghost the simple question, "What can we do for you?" I help witnesses communicate with the apparition, and surprisingly, people often learn much about its motives. I may also work with psychic practitioners to gain insight as to why the ghost is there. I think of it as a kind of diplomacy process.

Communication tends to be effective because often apparitions simply have messages to deliver or want to express their desire to stay in a place associated with their life. The ghost may express fear of moving on into the unknown. In most cases some resolution can be reached in the process of counseling the ghost.

The method works well even if the determination is that there is no ghost. However, witnesses often can't accept this conclusion. I use the talking-with-the-dead method as a kind of placebo. When the apparition seems to be symbolic of issues in the family, the ultimate goal of resolution is to get the folks into counseling.

On the other hand, if the apparition is non-conscious, as in a haunting, talking to it is about as effective as talking to your television. Nonetheless, the talking method may still work as a placebo to convince witnesses that the ghost is gone, which shuts down whatever process allows them to perceive the imprint.

INTERVIEW THE GHOST

IF AFTER YOU'VE EXPLAINED ALL POSSIBILITIES and you conclude that you're dealing with an apparition, remember that ghosts are people, too. Personality and intelligence don't change after death. Living people are often willing to talk things out—so are apparitions.

Involve witnesses in the communication with their ghosts. This empowers them, which diminishes fear and other adverse reactions. The witnesses are having the experience of perceiving the ghost, so it stands to reason that the witnesses are best able to communicate with it. A skilled psychic practitioner can also be of great assistance in translating what the ghost has to say.

ASK QUESTIONS

COMMUNICATION WITH GHOSTS IS MOST EFFECTIVE when the interview process is utilized. Tell witnesses or the psychic to ask questions like, "Who are you?", "What do you want?", and "What can I do to help you?" The objective is to learn what motivates the apparition to be in the house or building in the first place. Asking questions often get direct answers which surprise the people involved—including the ghosts!.

WHAT GHOSTS WANT

AS WITH LIVING PEOPLE, WHAT GHOSTS WANT can vary considerably. Many believe that ghosts "don't know they're dead." That some people would be in denial of their deaths is to be expected, since denial of health problems is common when people learn they have a terminal illness. An apparition may be in denial of death and may argue about ownership of the house, for example.

I have investigated cases in which the ghosts were aware of their state. The communications usually came through psychics and average folks. One of the best cases I had with verifiable information about the apparition came from a preteen having daily conversations with the ghost. While he was no psychic, the ghost had easily established a connection with the boy.

Use the communication process to learn details about the apparition and its motives. Ask the ghost questions to clarify its behavior. For example, in one case the ghost had unintentionally frightened a two-year-old child, which seriously affected the rest of the family. They were terrified. In the communication process, the ghost apologized profusely, saying he "liked kids" and was ecstatic that the child could see him. He just didn't realize he would frighten the child and the family so much.

People often blame the ghost for the clumsiness they experience in the face of the fear of seeing it. People have reported to me that "the ghost pushed me down the stairs." On examination, it was clear the individual fell when startled by the ghost, who was in sight but not close enough to push. The fall was a result of being startled and was not intentionally instigated by the apparition.

IGNORE THE GHOST

SOMETIMES WITNESSES perceived the apparition many times before they acknowledged its presence. They ignored the ghost. Like most people, apparitions probably go away when ignored. On the other hand, it may be pretty disconcerting for a discarnate entity to be ignored and he might decide to try to get the attention

Author at the Presidio Officer's Club, San Francisco.

of the living by attempting to interact more often.

It's rare for apparitions to be able to move objects. They must learn to exert mind over matter ability. In some cases, moving items is a sign of an escalation of events. The apparition tries harder and harder to get some kind of attention. In such cases, it's generally because the ghost has something particularly important to communicate or to ask of the living.

Witness reactions run from indifference to fear and frustration as the activity escalates. Often witnesses misinterpret the ghost's actions, thinking he wished them harm when in fact he only wanted to talk.

Push Lightly

Be watchful when asking people to participate in communication attempts with the ghost. If they are afraid, that fear may grow when pushed too hard to "talk" to the entity. The very idea that they should ask the ghost questions might frighten them even more. Remind witnesses that with rare exception, ghosts can't hurt them physically—or psychically. The only is the fear that they feel.

Humor

Humor is a great way to defeat fear, anger, and frustration. So interject a little humor. I'm not suggesting that you laugh at the ghost or make fun of her—although this can be a way to drive off some entities. I am suggesting that you be lighthearted and a little playful. Most people have a sense of humor—including the dead ones.

Listen and Learn

Take in the information the ghost provides in response to your questions. If the ghost wants something that is within the power of the witnesses or the investigative team to provide, go ahead and do it. Use common sense, however. Explain your motives to the ghost. Often the ghost leaves when witnesses try to help it out, even when they don't succeed.

Sometimes the ghost wants to help the witnesses, especially when it is a deceased family member. I've had cases in which the ghost wants to be friendly and helpful even though there's no relationship between the living and the apparition. In one case, the teenager communicating with the ghost claimed she was helping with his homework—his grades actually improved.

As the communication process proceeds witnesses can shift what they want the investigators to achieve. I've found that after the fear is gone and the motivations of the ghost are known, the people don't necessarily want the apparition to leave. As the tone of the case changes, the living become curious about the ghost. They may even want to make friends with it.

PRIVACY

THE STICKIEST ISSUE MAY BE PRIVACY. Since the apparition can be anywhere in the building and potentially intrude upon the folks living there, ground rules need to be set up to make sure that the ghost is not "peeping." It's important to get across to the ghost that if he is to stay, the privacy of the living people must be respected.

TELL THE GHOST TO LEAVE

ASKING THE GHOST TO leave will generally WORK, especially when the time is taken to explain how and why having her stick around bothers everyone and increases their stress. Like most living people, most ghosts are reasonable.

Sometimes an apparition is stubborn and refuses to leave, in spite of understanding how damaging his presence is to the people living in the place. In these cases, the living people must become firm, take control, and tell the ghost to leave in no uncertain terms. If that doesn't work, a psychic may be able to push it "to the light" or otherwise drive off the ghost.

If nothing I've suggested thus far works, the next step is to exert your personal control and demand that the ghost leave. Even though ignoring the ghost in the beginning of the process may escalate its activity, after the communication process is underway and the entity shows itself to be unreasonable, you might try being rude and ignoring him. Hopefully, the apparition will get bored and take off. Alternatively, you may be able to shift your own psychic processes to shut down receiving the ghost's signal.

In extreme cases, you might treat the unwelcome apparition like any other obnoxious house guest and insult him into leaving. I've had success by doing things the ghost doesn't like, such as playing loud music. I've also had success by telling the ghost bad knock-knock jokes, which was an idea suggested by a five-year-old child. This can be thought of as the technique of annoying the ghost out of the house. Sometimes sound and light equipment will frighten off the ghost, which I think of as a "scientific ritual."

BANISHING RITUALS

VETERAN BRITISH PARANORMAL FIELD RESEARCHER Tony Cornell suggests making up a ritual the witnesses can believe in. In one case, he advised mixing salt, bleach, and soil from around the house, then pouring the mixture in front of the doors to the house so the ghost couldn't come in. Methods such as this do seem to work.

These techniques probably have no actual affect on apparitions. But remember that ghost are presumably deceased people. Apparitions generally react the same way living people do, so when they believe a treatment has validity, they're likely to react to it in the same way as living people do.

VISUALIZATION

IF THE APPARITION SEEMS TO HAVE SETTLED IN despite your efforts to dislodge it, you might try having witnesses work with visualization. Psychics have suggested that you can protect yourself against outside psychic influences and block out psi signals by visualizing a protective wall, light, or force field around you. Visualizing certain colors around you, such as a purple or white light, or your favorite colors can also be helpful. Instruct witnesses to visualize the light or colors as a bubble around them that reflects outward anything hitting it. Witnesses can experiment with using actual mirrors or lights in the room to help focus.

Instruct witnesses to expand out the protective force field to enclose their house to block psi signals from coming in to it. In one case, a woman having problems with a verbally abusive ghost had difficulties in visualizing the force field surrounding her whole house. I suggested that she enclose the ghost in an

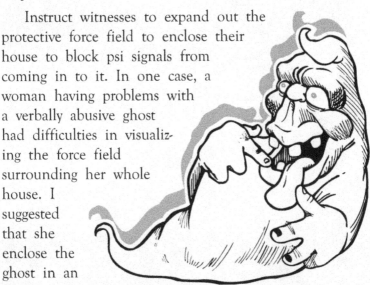

imaginary bell jar, then simply move the jar outside the house with him in it, and to warn him not to come back or suffer the same treatment. It was successful.

Sometimes rituals of a religious or cultural nature, such as blessing your house with holy water or smudging the house with smoldering sage, are effective. Generally, such effects work only when witnesses—and their ghosts—believe in the power of the ritual.

Choose your intervention and resolution tools carefully. Don't rush out to get a psychic or go running to an exorcist to cleanse the location. Such rituals can create psychological havoc and may exacerbate the root cause of the phenomena. Look for normal explanations first. Then assess the psychological and symbolic content of the case. You can always talk to the ghost later. When the witnesses realize an apparition can't harm them, many have little problem coexisting with their ghost—so long as the ghost respects their privacy.

26

RESOLVING HAUNTINGS

ESOLUTION IS TRICKY WITH HAUNTINGS because they are apparent environmental recordings. Hauntings tend to be more annoying and disconcerting than fear-inducing, especially once witnesses understand the dynamics and cause. When witnesses realize that no intelligent ghost is involved, they can still be upset by the occurrences, and counseling may be necessary. The content of the imprints may be related to emotionally charged—and often negative—events. Apparition and poltergeist cases tend to be easier to deal with than are hauntings because of their interactive nature.

Do Historical Research

HAUNTINGS APPEAR TO BE REPLAYS OF RECORDED IMPRINTS of people, animals, and events that occurred in the past. They may have occurred or been present in the haunted building, or in a building that once stood on the spot, or on the land before anything was built there. Because hauntings relate to past events, ghost hunters dig into the history of past inhabitants of the building and do historical research on the property and the surrounding area. This generally involves checking county records and possibly visiting the local historical society. There will be times when you can't find anything that seems significant enough to have left an imprint. However, murders, battles, and violent events are not needed to create a place memory. Strong emotions of an individual who lived at that spot may be sufficient. Hauntings are not fully understood. There are some conditions that appear to correlate with the imprint, and there may be other environmental factors that we've yet to uncover or connect that trigger the making of imprints.

MINOR REPLAYS

HAUNTINGS OFTEN EXHIBIT ONLY MINOR REPLAYS, such as footsteps pacing a hallway or sounds of pots and pans rattling in the kitchen. Sometimes witnesses report experiencing sensations of a cat or dog in the house when no pets live there and no one has witnessed an animal apparition.

Winchester Mystery House in San Jose, California.

You may be surprised to learn that positive events are more commonly recorded than negative ones. It's rare however for ghost hunters to be called into investigate a neutral or positive haunt. Imagine getting a call from a witnesses who says, "Our house is haunted. We constantly feel good in one spot in the house and don't know why." Because witnesses tend to seek help only with frightening or depressing or annoying hauntings, the public perception is that most hauntings are negative events.

UNDERSTANDING IS KEY

I HAD A CASE WHERE THE IMPRINT was of two people making love. The haunting consisted of the sounds of the couple having sex, as heard from the next bedroom. As is sometimes the case in hauntings, the people who caused the impression—the previous owners of the home—were still alive. The new residents called because they were a little unnerved being woken up almost every night by sounds of loud love-making. They wanted to know what was going on and why.

Understanding the situation resolved the case. The sleepless couple moved their bed into the bedroom where the imprint was located. Because they only perceived the imprint from the next bedroom, they suffered no further disturbances.

Hauntings are like background noise. I encourage folks to think of them as they do the background. noise we hear when living near a highway. We quickly learn to screen out the traffic noise so that we don't consciously hear it anymore—until someone says, "How can you live here with all that noise?" Then we hear it again briefly, until it fades back into the background. We have to learn to screen it out all over again. People have varying success with getting used to noise from hauntings. For example, could *you* get used to the sounds of people making love at 3 a.m. in the next room?

CLEANSE THE LOCATION

SOME PSYCHICS HAVE HAD SUCCESS CLEANSING A LOCATION by doing visualizations that seem to affect the energy of the haunting. I've found it interesting to watch a magnetic reading drop from significantly higher than normal for the location to next to nothing in the short time the psychic worked the cleansing visualization. Sometimes multiple cleansings are required because the patterns of the imprinted recordings and the magnetic readings varied too much for one cleansing to be totally effective.

I have successfully used magnets to eliminate the anomalous readings on detection devices, which I take as evidence of having cleansed the energy. Small but powerful, rare earth magnets are available from Radio Shack and a variety of internet sources. These can be placed in the locations where the hauntings occur. I've had success using a powerful electromagnet, such as a Video/Audio Tape Eraser, also known as a Bulk Tape Eraser, to disrupt anomalous magnetic fields as measured by detection devices. Here again, more than one application is sometimes necessary.

I don't know why this works. But then I don't know where anomalous magnetic fields comes from either. Perhaps these techniques have a placebo effect. Regardless, they do work. Other rituals, such as using sound and light devices, can be effective—also possibly a result of the placebo effect. With medical placebos, believing the treatment is effective seems to be the critical variable. Similarly, when witnesses *believe* the haunting is over, unconscious processes seem to make sure this is the case and the experiences cease.

The shielding techniques often used in apparition cases may work to dispel hauntings. Apparently, people learn to screen out psychic information in the same way that they learn to screen out input from an apparition.

Another technique that has had much success in haunting cases is to record over the haunt. The method is easy. Hold a positive, emotionally charged event at the site, like a big party or game playing—something that would generate good vibes. The objective is for the positive emotions to neutralize or record over the old place memories that constitute the haunting. Of course, you could potentially be recording a new imprint that will be perceived by future inhabitants of the house.

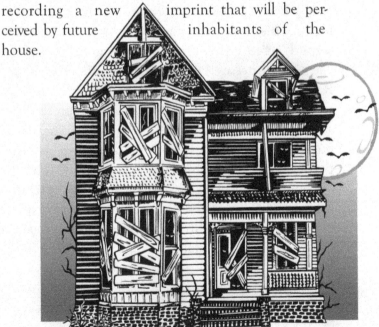

27

BANISHING RITUALS

HE BELIEF SYSTEM OF WITNESSES ought to be explored in all three of our major phenomena—poltergeists, apparitions, and hauntings. It is important to explain the findings of your investigation in terms of the beliefs and cultural backgrounds of the witnesses. Tying your explanation to witnesses beliefs is especially important when witnesses are resistance to particular ideas. This does not mean that ghost hunters should agree to "get rid of a demons" simply because witnesses believe demons are present. Rather ghost hunters should work with the belief to understand why the phenomena represents itself as a demon and why the psychological needs of those involved are expressing themselves as demons. By speaking their language, so to speak, and looking at events through witnesses' beliefs, the investigator might be better able to explain an experience to witnesses and help them accept that it is not really the work of demons, and that there may be no conscious entity present at all.

STUDY MYTHOLOGY

IN MOST CASES, ANOMALOUS EVENTS are not indicative of an evil presence. When witnesses express concern that the presence is demonic you need to trace this concern to its roots if the case is to be successfully resolved. As part of your training as an investigator, I advise that you study anthropological and historical religious literature. Not all religions believe in the existence of Heaven and Hell, or in angels and demons, although most do recognize some form of "evil" as existing. You can gain an understanding of how such religious concepts impact people in various cultures by reading cultural anthropology.

There are many books and articles available that deal with supernatural and magical beliefs in different cultures. Having an understanding of how different cultures view psychic experience, abilities, and ghostly phenomena proves helpful in many cases. Similarly, having an understanding of the history of the major religions will probably be quite eye-opening and will make you a better investigator.

When I am called into a case, I specifically make the point that, as a parapsychologist, I deal with the human mind—living or dead—and with how the mind interacts with the environment. Parapsychologists do not attempt to resolve such cases through a frame of reference involving demons. There is no evidence in parapsychological literature or in case reports to indicate that demons are responsible for typical psychic or psychological phenomena.

DISCLOSE

IF YOU FEEL THE NECESSITY to bring your personal
religious beliefs into the investigation, tell your potential clients in the initial interview. Make sure to
explain that these are your personal religious beliefs
and not the prevailing view of parapsychological
research. Never claim a scientific perspective if your
investigation is rooted in religious dogma. It is your
responsibility as a professional to not misrepresent
yourself and your perspective to the people calling
you for help. If you fail to do so, clients are likely
to sense your bias and they will not trust you or
your advice.

There have been many cases in which I had to
assume "cleanup duty" after unprofessional
demonologists, ghost hunters, or psychics made snap
judgments and proclaimed the presence of demons or
evil spirits, rather than to objectively explore what
was going on. Families were left even more frightened and often became distrustful of help that a
skilled investigator could offer. In some cases, the
perception of demons had normal explanations but
the demon-hunters had failed to looked for alternative explanations and fell back on their own biases
instead. As a result they diagnosed the cases as being
caused by the presence of evil beings when the
actual cause was a naturally occurring event, like
leaky and noisy pipes or a radio hidden behind a
radiator.

BANISHING RITUALS

BANISHING RITUALS CAN OFTEN BE EFFECTIVE but should
be used only after exploring the client's beliefs.
When the folks believe in the ritual's power and it
is compatible with their religious views, it is likely to

yield a positive effect. Even when a banishing ritual is effective in resolving the case, follow up counseling should be considered.

Misguided use of banishing rituals can sometimes cause the phenomena to escalate. In a poltergeist case, a religious rite could cause the agent's subconscious to decide it has to "prove" that the ritual is ineffective and the RSPK can increase as a result. If the investigator suggests, even unwittingly, that the agent is "possessed" the agent could perceive the ritual as directed against him or her, which could dramatically increase poltergeist activity.

On the other hand, in apparition cases there are two sides to every interaction. A banishing ritual could cause the witness to shut down perceptions of the ghost, but the apparition might still be present and perceived by others. On the other hand, if the apparition believes in the ritual's effectiveness, enacting it might scare him off.

SCIENCE AND RELIGION

WHETHER OR NOT A SCIENTIFIC-BASED INVESTIGATOR should bring in religious help is sometimes considered. In most cases I'd say no. However, when I find that the client's beliefs are strong, and I can find an appropriate cleric who is willing to work with me and who is not personally tied to religious dogma, then I will use this resource. I've had success using Catholic priests, Wiccans, and Rabbis over the years. Interestingly, I've gotten referrals from priests who identified a poltergeist or a haunting phenomena as the cause of the disturbance rather than the demon that the parishioners had assumed was present.

28

BE PROFESSIONAL

OU MAY HAVE SEEN ME ON A TELEVISION SHOW about ghosts or psychic phenomena. The cases investigated on national TV are not the typical ones that most people call me about.

Most people grappling with anomalous events don't want their neighbors to know they have a ghost or poltergeist, let alone the whole world. I promise confidentiality and anonymity in all cases, except when the clients have given permission to disclose their identity and the details of the case. I never bring in reporters, without first discussing it with my clients and getting their express permission. I always make sure to establish a clear understanding of how much of their personal details can be revealed.

When I write articles about cases, I include only as much detail as the clients permit. Cases can be written up with minimal personal details. Usually using only first names and witnesses' professions, if relevant, is workable. I may include the name of the town where the events occurred but never the street or neighborhood. I typically include general information about the family, such as having two kids. I give details of the case that help understand what happened, such as in which room the events took place. I am careful to exclude any details that would enable someone to track the witnesses down or to figure out who they are.

Cases I do with media fall generally into three categories. Most common are public sites, such as restaurants and historical sites willing to cooperate with the media. Second are cases where the clients are fully aware of the possible consequences of appearing on TV or being mentioned in articles and who are willing to cooperate. The final type of case is house- or family-based cases brought to me by the TV producers or publication. I am a bit leery about the cases brought to me by the media, however.

Before agreeing to work the case on a television show, I always thoroughly check out the public places to make sure that what's been reported to me has really happened and that it is not an "urban legend." Additionally, I carefully check out the witnesses' motivations and refuse cases in which I suspect that the motive is to gain publicity or money.

Be careful when working with television and print media to make sure that it is a legitimate show or publication. Ask what other shows or articles they've done on the same subject to get a feel for what angle they're going to take. Be aware that what's shot and the information taken in notes is subject to drastic editing. Sometimes how the story is covered will be changed before it is released. Always protect clients' privacy. It may be helpful read up on how to be a good interview subject and to sharpen your speaking skills so you come across intelligently.

Legal And Ethical Considerations

Never offer to provide psychological-type services if you are not licensed to do so. Be careful not to break anything when investigating someone's house. Make sure you don't make promises you can't keep.

You, the investigator, assume an ethical duty when accepting someone's call for help. My motto is: *Do your best and do your best to do no harm.* If you can't help the caller, say so and give a referral to someone who may be able to help. When you accept a case, focus on the needs of the witnesses and clients—and possibly the ghost. Gather data according to scientific guidelines to make an objective assessment. Remember why you've been called in—to help.

Make sure you explain the benefits of counseling in these situations, and offer suggestions as to how to get such help. Always treat people with respect— living and dead alike.

Charging Fees

If you charge a fee, make sure that you are offering a service and information that has value and are not simply a voyeur snooping around, hoping to "experience something." Be sure not to charge too much. Ghost hunting is not about getting rich. I recommend using a sliding scale. I have found that often the people most willing to pay are often the ones with the least money.

Some believe that charging anything at all is wrong. That's fine, and I applaud their willingness to work for free. Often, however, people don't use free advice, possibly because they only value something if they pay for it. Some investigators barter services.

There are ghost hunters who charge fees in the thousands of dollars for an investigation, justifying it with a list of expensive—but unnecessary—equipment. This cuts most people out of the can-I-get-help equation. It makes me wonder about their ethics and just what kind of services they're offering.

29

FINAL WORDS

E DISCERNING IN YOUR ASSESSMENT of the paranormal. Think of these experiences as part of normal experience. Ask many questions to find answers and to find the right questions to fit the answers in front of you.

Apparitions, poltergeists, and hauntings aren't everyday experiences. Nonetheless, enough people have reported such incidents that it's apparent that the phenomena are part of the human experience. I suspect that many more people than those who have reported them have had these types of experiences.

As a new investigator don't hesitate to seek outside advice from trained parapsychologists, psychologists, or transpersonal counselors who can address more than the psychic side of anomalous experiences.

Consult with experienced investigators when questions come up. Many investigators are more than willing to mentor less experienced ghost hunters.

Locate reputable research centers and organizations specializing in paranormal activity as resources where you can seek advice. If they cannot help you directly, they can refer you to professionals who can help. Be informed and check out practitioners and ghost hunting groups with reputable organizations such as the Rhine Research Center, the Parapsychology Foundation, the American Society for Psychical Research, and the Parapsychological Association.

I am a believer in some kind of channel of human perception and interaction that science hasn't yet figured out. Whether you agree with me or not, you probably agree that people experience a range of things labeled as *psychic* or *paranormal*. Keep in mind, however, that labels can be deceiving and can themselves be factors that limit exploration and understanding.

Science progresses by asking questions and seeking answers, not by shunting aside areas of human experience that don't fit with our beliefs or make sense. Too much pushing aside of ideas has gone on in the history of our civilization. Parapsychology is the study of unexplained human experiences. Parapsychologists are the only folks conducting controlled research into anomalous phenomena, like apparitions, hauntings and poltergeists. Skeptics bring skepticism—which is useful, but they add little to our knowledge.

The field of parapsychology started with the formation of the Society for Psychical Research in 1882. Some have asked what, if anything, has been learned. We've learned about psychological variables and beliefs that affect psychic abilities. We've learned that geomagnetic fields affect the human brain and seem to have had something to do with causing hallucinations and possibly enhancing or blocking psychic experiences. We've learned that there's an apparent window of Local Sidereal Time, during which people seem to be more psychic. We've learned that there are other natural causes for apparition and haunting experiences, such as low-frequency sound waves. We're learning more and more about anomalous experiences and phenomena each year.

Parapsychology has done well considering what is studied and how much the developing ideas, concepts, and techniques of other fields are needed to understand what may be going on during paranormal activity. New knowledge gained from quantum physics, psychology, and biology is advancing parapsychology.

As a science, parapsychology needs a boost. With ideas and innovations from other sciences, combined with a move to look for real-life patterns in these experiences, we may be on the verge of substantiating psi as "real."

From cases of poltergeists, apparitions, and hauntings, I've learned how people's beliefs, thought processes, psychological makeups, and interpersonal interactions shape psi experiences. It's been a slow road, but we're making headway.

Laugh A Lot

WITHOUT A SENSE OF HUMOR, ghost hunters can become susceptible to being obsessed by subjective paranormal experiences. The movie *Ghost busters* brought this point home to many ghost hunters. Laughing at the full range of human experience, and at ourselves as ghost hunters, can help to keep perspective. Psychic experience is a part of the normal range of human experience. Enjoy it—learn from the experiences and what they say about life. Interject humor into otherwise fearful experiences. You have nothing to fear from psi phenomena except your own fear.

When you get a twinge of apprehension, learn to say, "I ain't 'fraid o' no ghosts...or poltergeists...or hauntings...or precognitive experiences...or the unknown."

GHOST HUNTER CHECKLIST

Conduct an in-depth interview before launching an investigation.

Confirm that the phenomena is still going on, that there is more than one witness, and that there's a need to investigate.

Explore normal causes for the reported phenomena *before* launching an investigation.

Don't go alone.

Bring equipment you may need, especially recording devices, such as camera, tape recorder, video camera, paper and pen.

Avoid publicity and debunkers.

Interview all witnesses on site, when possible. Interview all non-witness residents.

Ask more questions; interview witnesses and non-witness residents again.

Seek normal explanations for the individual incidents and the overall case.

Look for relationships between the people and the events.

Gather data with detection devices, including psychics and intuitives. Use the Anomalous Experiences Checklist.

Observe. Observe. Observe!

Discuss the data gathered—from interviews, detectors, sensitives and investigators' opinions—to make an assessment.

Develop a follow-up plan, including further visits, education, and resolution techniques—or doing nothing more.

Write your report—if for no other reason than to keep track of your cases.

RECOMMENDED BOOKS

Auerbach, Loyd. *ESP, Hauntings and Poltergeists: A Parapsychologist's Handbook.* Warner Books, 1986.

Auerbach, Loyd. *Mind Over Matter.* Kensington Books, 1996.

Baker, Robert A. and Joe Nickell. *Missing Pieces: How to Investigate Ghosts, UFOs, Psychics & Other Mysteries.* Prometheus Books, 1992.

Broughton, Richard. *Parapsychology: The Controversial Science.* Ballantine Books, 1991.

Cornell, Tony. *Investigating the Paranormal.* Helix Press, 2002.

Houran, James and Rense Lange, (eds). *Hauntings and Poltergeists: Multidisciplinary Perspectives.* McFarland, 2001.

Irwin, Harvey J. *An Introduction to Parapsychology,* 3rd edition. McFarland, 1999.

Radin, Dean I. *The Conscious Universe: The Scientific Truth of Psychic Phenomena.* HarperEdge, HarperSanFrancisco, 1997.

Rogo, D. Scott. *An Experience of Phantoms.* Taplinger Publishing Co., 1974.

Rogo, D. Scott. *The Poltergeist Experience.* Penguin Books, 1979.

Rogo, D. Scott. *Life After Death: The Case for Survival of Bodily Death.* The Aquarian Press, 1986.

Roll, William G. *The Poltergeist.* Scarecrow Press, 1976.

Moss, Thelma and Gertrude R. Schmeidler. "Quantitative Investigation of a 'Haunted House' with Sensitives and a Control Group." *Journal of the American Society for Psychical Research,* vol. 62, October 1968, pp. 399-410.

Tyrrell, G.N.M. *Apparitions.* Collier Books, 1963.

Underwood, Peter. *The Ghost Hunter's Guide.* Javelin Books, 1986.

Wolman, Benjamin, and Montague Ullman, Montague, Laura Dale, Gertrude Schmeidler, (eds). *Handbook of Parapsychology.* McFarland, 1986.

PROFESSOR PARANORMAL

Loyd Auerbach is a mentalist and psychic entertainer. He is also the Director of the Office of Paranormal Investigations, a consulting Editor and columnist for FATE Magazine, a professor at JFK University and President of the Psychic Entertainers Association, a past President of the California Society for Psychic Study, and co-founder of the Paranormal Research Organization (paranormal-research.org), which is aimed at networking and bringing professional standards to paranormal investigators. He holds a masters in parapsychology and has been investigating the Paranormal for over 25 years. Loyd Auerbach is an international expert on ghosts, poltergeists and psychic experience.

Visit Professor Paranormal s website at mindreader.com or contact him via email at esper@california.com or by phone at the Office of Paranormal Investigations, 415-249-9275.

Printed in the USA
CPSIA information can be obtained
at www.ICGtesting.com
JSHW012051140824
68134JS00035B/3380

9 781579 510671